T0369079

The Physics of Soccer:

Using Math and Science to Improve Your Game

DEJI
BADIRU

iUniverse, Inc.
New York   Bloomington

iUniverse books may be ordered through booksellers or by contacting:

iUniverse
1663 Liberty Drive
Bloomington, IN 47403
www.iuniverse.com
1-800-Authors (1-800-288-4677)

ISBN: 978-1-4401-9224-1 (sc)
ISBN: 978-1-4401-9225-8 (ebook)
ISBN: 978-1-4401-9226-5 (hc)

Printed in the United States of America

iUniverse rev. date: 01/04/2010

With contributions from:

Ade Badiru
Mechanical engineer and former elite soccer star
> He played competitive soccer on several elite and select soccer teams for over twelve years in Oklahoma and now plays recreationally in Detroit, Michigan.

TJ Badiru
Former high school varsity soccer star
> He played competitive soccer on several elite teams in Oklahoma, Tennessee, and Ohio. He played varsity soccer at West High School, Knoxville, Tennessee, and Beavercreek High School, Beavercreek, Ohio.

Anota Ijaduola
Physics instructor at Monmouth College, Monmouth, Illinois

John Brian Peacock
Professor of engineering and former soccer teammate of the author.
> Dr. Peacock was a soccer player, coach, and referee for more than sixty years. His last competitive game was when he was in his late fifties.

===

Photographs:
Photos of soccer demo moves courtesy of Melissa Witkovsky. Other photos are from the author's personal and family photo collections.

Illustrations and line drawings:
By author (© Adedeji Badiru) except where credits are noted

Front Cover Photo Credit:
iStockphoto.com, Flying-Soccer –Player (File# 1449729)

Titles in ABICS Publications book series on recreational, educational, motivational, and personal development books:

- Books for home, work, and leisure
  www.abicspublications.com

- *Getting Things Done through Project Management*
  by Deji Badiru (2009)

- *The Physics of Soccer: Using Math and Science to Improve Your Game*
  by Deji Badiru (2010)

The Physics of Soccer:
Using Math and Science to Improve Your Game

Deji Badiru

Books for home, work, and leisure

ABICS Publications
A Division of
AB International Consulting
Services

The Physics of Soccer: Using Math and Science to Improve Your Game is dedicated to the spirit of sportsmanship, not only in soccer, but in all sports.

The book is also dedicated to the collective nations of Africa in commemoration of 2010 Soccer World Cup in South Africa.

Contents

Preface

The title of this book, *The Physics of Soccer: Using Math and Science to Improve Your Game,* was selected to serve two purposes, figuratively and literally. The literal interpretation of the title conveys the direct functional role of physics as a scientific tool in the game of soccer. The figurative interpretation conveys the fact that the "physics" of something is often used to refer to how something is done, as in how to practice and execute the game of soccer. For comparison, the book *Factory Physics*[1] by Wallace Hopp and Mark L. Spearman (2008) presents fundamental how-to processes of manufacturing, including cycle time, throughput, quality, capacity, work-in-process, inventory, and reliability. The authors describe twenty-two laws (i.e., physics) for manufacturing that help managers better understand production, control cost, improve performance, and manage workers in a manufacturing plant. *The Physics of Soccer* similarly seeks to improve understanding, control, performance, and player management on the soccer playing field. In effect, the physics behind the game of soccer helps us to understand the game better and makes it possible to play the game more efficiently. Efficiency is defined as the ratio of output (result) to input (effort).

The chapters in *The Physics of Soccer* are Importance of STEM (science, technology, engineering, and mathematics) in Sports; Physics and Motion; Energy and Work; Soccer Basics; Soccer Motion Analysis; Soccer Field Generalship; Physics of the Soccer Foot; Brian Peacock's Soccer Training Clinic; Brian Peacock's Seventeen Steps of Soccer Training; Soccer Calculations; Soccer Trivia; and Scientific

---

1. Hopp, Wallace J. and Mark L. Spearman, *Factory Physics,* 3rd ed., McGraw-Hill International Edition, McGraw-Hill/Irwin, Boston, 2008.

Management of Soccer. An appendix is also provided with units of measurement and conversion factors.

Who Should Read this Book

Although the primary focus of *The Physics of Soccer: Using Math and Science to Improve Your Game* is on adolescent soccer players, younger players will enjoy it also as an introductory preparation for how they may approach soccer in later years. It is never too early to introduce players to the beauty of mathematical and scientific reasoning and their applications.

Soccer coaches, soccer parents, and league administrators can also benefit from the book. For this reason, specific paragraphs are included in the book to address the interests of these groups. Soccer moms and soccer spouses can particularly benefit from the chapters on soccer basics and examples, which are presented in a simple and illustrative format. Similarly, soccer grandparents will be interested in this book as a gift to grandchildren. Even professional soccer players will find the book to be of great value because it can help them understand the physics behind what they do so well. It is hoped that this book can help increase general awareness of science and technology as something we see and use every day, particularly in sports. *The Physics of Soccer* can also help to demystify STEM so that young soccer players can readily embrace it as a career path.

Author's Credentials for the Book

Author Deji Badiru has multiple years of experience with soccer, as listed below:
- Over forty years as a soccer player
- Twenty-five years as a soccer dad
- Five years as youth soccer coach

- Three years as adult soccer coach
- One adult soccer season as soccer husband while his wife, Iswat, played briefly with the "Femme Fatale" adult female soccer team in Norman, Oklahoma, in the mid-1990s.

On the technical side, the author's credentials span the following:
- Over thirty years as an engineering educator
- Registered professional engineer (PE)
- Certified Project Management Professional (PMP)
- Member of Nigerian Academy of Engineers
- Fellow of the Institute of Industrial Engineers
- Award-winning author, educator, researcher, and administrator

Acknowledgments

I thank **Candi Cross** (www.candicross.com) for her initial copyediting of this book. Her editorial services substantively improved the quality of the manuscript.

I greatly thank **Donna Mullenax**, who did a thorough technical review of the manuscript. She caught all my physics faux pas in the manuscript. Whatever errors remain (if there are any) are entirely due to the author's own flaws.

I also thank members of the **Jeremy Slagley** family for their review of the finished manuscript. Their interest and dedication to the sport provided unparalleled inspiration for several segments of this book.

I thank the entire **editorial staff of iUniverse** for their editorial proficiency and professionalism throughout the production of this book.

My gratitude also goes to my teammates and soccer associates of the past, who created game scenarios from which I could draw examples and illustrations for this book.

Of course, the direct contributions of my soccer-playing sons, Ade and Tunji (TJ), are paternally acknowledged and greatly appreciated. **Tunji** was the model in most of the photos used in this book. **Ade** used his own perspectives as a soccer player, coach, and organizer to suggest structural adjustments that improved the quality of this book. He also posed as model for many of the demonstration photos in the book. Of special note are the support and contributions of my daughter, **Abi**, who always provided a loud cheering voice during her brothers' soccer games. She also played one year of recreational youth soccer in the mid-1980s in Norman, Oklahoma.

Special thanks go to my wife, **Iswat**, for her usual support in typing many parts of this manuscript. During my soccer-playing days, she was always on the sideline, cautiously supportive and shouting words of caution about not getting hurt. She finally forced me to retire from competitive soccer at the age of forty-five, asserting that it was no longer safe for me to go chasing a ball around and getting knocked down by hefty and burly opponents. Although I initially protested with a dissenting opinion, aged and achy muscles finally compelled me to comply. Due to my regular daytime, full-time job, this book was written in night and weekend sessions that stretched over many years. It takes an understanding spouse to cope with such prolonged diversion. Thanks, Iswat!

Introduction

The Physics of Soccer: Using Math and Science to Improve Your Game teaches soccer players to view the game from a scientific and intellectual point of view rather than just a physical undertaking. The author designed the book to be fun and yet technically stimulating for young readers. The book helps soccer players to accomplish the following:

- Use their mind to gain an edge over opponents
- Apply knowledge of STEM (science, technology, engineering, and mathematics) to everyday problems, particularly sports
- Critically assess soccer game scenarios and make appropriate field-based decisions based on science
- Assess the capabilities of teammates and opponents from a scientific viewpoint
- Capitalize on the geometry of the field of play and respective locations and placements of other players
- Use nonverbal "communication" to direct or influence the motion of teammates and opponents
- View the field of play as a system of people (players, coaches, referees, spectators, supporters, detractors), objects (soccer ball, the pitch, goal posts), and the environment, whose respective behaviors are governed by the laws of science
- Quickly assess the implications of directional motions of opponents and teammates on the field of play
- Enjoy the applications of physics to the game of soccer and leverage the enjoyment to build interest in further study of science

- Use the team organization, cooperation, and spirit learned in soccer to develop other life skills in group settings

Because boys and girls now play soccer widely, the masculine terms "he," "his," and "him" are used in this book in an inclusive context to denote both genders. The soccer narratives and instructions in *The Physics of Soccer* apply equally to both male and female players.

Also, because soccer is such an international sport, it is instructive for readers to be familiar with the various terminologies that may be encountered. Thus, this book, when appropriate, mentions football as well as metric measurement units commonly used in many parts of the world.

Learn Soccer, Have Fun, and Be Happy

An important aspect of playing the team sport of soccer is the camaraderie that kids develop while learning the game and having fun. This philosophy is aptly conveyed by professional soccer player Freddy Adu, who says, "I just want to get out there and play and have fun. After all, when I'm on a soccer field, that's when I'm at my happiest."[2]

Soccer is a game for everyone. Kids should learn, practice, and enjoy the game for fun and health. In-class learning, as shown in the introductory Figure I.1, should be implemented on the field.

---

2.   http://thinkexist.com/quotes/freddy_adu/

Figure I.1: Intellectual learning of soccer (Introduction)

Tell me, and I forget;
Show me, and I remember;
Involve me, and I understand.

—Chinese Proverb

As the Chinese proverb above suggests, classroom briefing, lectures, visual demonstration, and book learning must be transferred to the practice level and, eventually, executed in actual games. The contents of this book represent one of the stages of the tripartite process of learning and excelling at soccer.

If a kid loves soccer, we should try to use that passion as a vehicle to introduce science and math to the kid. Conversely, the inherent curiosity and excitement of STEM can be leveraged to enhance the game of soccer.

From an intellectual perspective, learning physics may be a source of fun and happiness as evidenced by the laudable quote below:

"I would get a Ph.D. in physics even if I made minimum wage afterwards. It's what I want to do."

—Zach Gault, physics major, Wright State University, Dayton, Ohio

This is a very impressive statement that affirms the enthusiasm of a young person about the subject of physics. Hopefully, *The Physics of Soccer* will get other young people equally excited about the subject. Popular science books about physicists can also fuel the interest of readers about the importance of science in our daily lives.[3,4]

The comical referee in Figure I.2 is designed to provide some comic relief before we get into serious discussions of The Physics of Soccer.

Figure I.2: Comical Referee – Where's the ball? I dunno!

3.   Watts, Duncan J., *Six Degrees: The Science of a Connected Age*, W. W. Norton & Co., New York, NY, 2003.
4.   Bak, Per, *How Nature Works: The Science of Self-Organized Criticality*, Copernicus/Springer-Verlag, New York, NY, 1999.

Chapter 1
Importance of STEM in Sports

"My interest is in the future because I am going to spend the rest of my life there."

—Charles F. Kettering

Physics[5] explains the past, the present, and the future. Physics is the science of matter and energy, and the interactions between the two (Halliday et al. 2007). The physics of soccer is addressed as a topic in this book, both literally and figuratively. The literal part relates to the science and computational aspects of soccer. The figurative part presents physics informally as the process of accomplishing soccer-related actions. The approach of this book helps players to develop more as cerebral participants rather than just brawny athletes.

Whether it is called *soccer*, *football*, or *the world's game*, the game of soccer is fun and has been called the most popular sport in the world. The game of soccer is about motion. Physics is about the laws of motion, and it can be applied to ball games (Daish 1972, Adair 2002, Gay 2004). Putting soccer and physics together is one way to appreciate the high-speed aspects of the sport. One purpose of this book is to introduce some basic mathematics and science concepts in an interesting, useful, and engaging way.

Soccer builds character. The game extends and builds positive attributes in players. From physical and mental alertness, teamwork, sportsmanship, selflessness, and leadership to good work ethics, the game of soccer helps players to develop as a total person as they prepare for the challenges of the future.

Orientation of Soccer Toward STEM

STEM[6] is an acronym for "science, technology, engineering, and mathematics." It is a motivational philosophy that uses technical math and science subject areas to develop a better understanding of our world, environment, operational processes, and how things work. STEM prepares youth for the challenges they will face in college, professional careers, and the workplace. National forecasts have projected up to a 30 percent increase in science and technical occupations in the

---

5. http://en.wikipedia.org/wiki/Physics
6. www.stemedcoalition.org/

2

coming decades. In order to be well-rounded and be prepared for the challenges of the future at home or at work, we must embrace STEM enthusiastically. Using sports as a vehicle for building enthusiasm in STEM is a creative and unique way to get the attention of youths. Sport is one thing that most youths engage in enthusiastically, and we can leverage it into building an interest in STEM. Several states are stemming up (pun intended) to the challenge of STEM by creating incubator programs to give youths an early start in science, technology, engineering, and mathematics. At the professional level, STEM-oriented publications are emerging in business, education, industry, and management (Badiru 2009). On the education side, of noteworthy mention is the aggressive effort of STEM Education Coalition,[7] whose objectives are echoed in the shaded display below:

7. www.stemedcoalition.org/content/objectives/Default.aspx

STEM Education Coalition

The STEM Education Coalition works aggressively to raise awareness in Congress, the administration, and other organizations about the critical role that STEM education plays in enabling the United States to remain the economic and technological leader of the global marketplace of the twenty-first century. The Coalition advocates for strengthening of STEM-related programs for educators and students and increased federal investments in STEM education. We also support robust federal investments in basic scientific research to inspire current and future generations of young people to pursue careers in STEM fields. Members of the STEM Coalition believe that our nation must improve the way our students learn science, mathematics, technology, and engineering and that the business, education, and STEM communities must work together to achieve this goal.

Coalition Objectives

1. Strengthen effective STEM education programs at all levels—K–12, undergraduate, graduate, continuing ed, vocational, informal—at the National Science Foundation, the U.S. Department of Education, and other federal agencies with STEM-related programs.

2. Encourage national elected officials and key opinion leaders to recognize and bring attention to the critical role that STEM education plays in U.S. competitiveness and our future economic prosperity.

3. Support new and innovative initiatives that will help improve the content knowledge, skills, and professional development of the K–12 STEM teacher workforce and informal educators and improve the resources available in STEM classrooms and other learning environments.

4. Support new and innovative initiatives to recruit and retain highly skilled STEM teachers.

5. Support new and innovative initiatives to encourage more of our best and brightest students, especially those from underrepresented or disadvantaged groups, to study in STEM fields.

6. Support increased federal investment in educational research to determine effective STEM teaching and learning methods.

7. Encourage better coordination of efforts among federal agencies that provide STEM education programs.

8. Support new and innovative initiatives that encourage partnerships between state and local educators, colleges, universities, museums, science centers, and the business, science, and technology communities that will improve STEM education.

Notable state-level STEM models can be found in Ohio,[8] Michigan,[9] and Minnesota.[10] The Dayton Regional STEM School[11] in Beavercreek, Ohio, is one of several specialized STEM schools established around the state of Ohio. It represents a good educational model for introducing youths to STEM education as early as possible.

8. www.usinnovation.org/state/pdf_stem/STEMEdOhio08.pdf
9. www.usinnovation.org/state/pdf_stem/STEMEdMichigan08.pdf
10. www.usinnovation.org/state/pdf_stem/STEMEdMinnesota08.pdf
11. daytonstemschool.org/

Started in fall 2009, the intensive science-oriented high school enrolls almost one hundred ninth-graders from school districts in the region. The STEM school will add grades each year until it reaches an enrollment of six hundred students in grades six through twelve. The idea of a STEM school is to steer young talents toward high-tech careers, which will be in demand in the future. The governor of Ohio conveys this fact from an executive viewpoint in this 2009 statement:

Our investment in STEM education is one of the most essential investments we can make, not only for our students, but for the future of the state of Ohio.

—Ted Strickland, governor of Ohio

The future workforce will consist of more knowledge workers than production floor workers. Those who will thrive in the future work environment are those with STEM-oriented education and aptitude. We are already seeing the emergence of noncontact service interactions. Think of online airline check-in, virtual boarding passes, PayPal, and a myriad of other examples. Goods and services can now easily be ordered and delivered via the Internet. Nintendo's Wii demonstrates that you can have physical activities and competitive game experience without physical contact and brutality. Wii was developed using higher-order STEM tools and techniques. The game of soccer, inasmuch as it is still played physically on the field, should take advantage of the intellectual tools, knowledge, and techniques of STEM. This book plays a role in that goal.

Although STEM philosophy focuses on technical subject areas, it should be understood that those technical areas function best only when the humanities are integrated into them. It is the view of this author that STEM works best when we also appreciate the social science areas that help us to build interpersonal skills needed for team activities, such as playing soccer.

Growth of Soccer in the United States

Even though soccer is still in a lull in the United States, the country should not despair. Soccer is growing fast in the United States both as a participative sport and as a family spectator sport. U.S. families now regularly huddle around the TV to watch international soccer games. On July 14, 2009, President Obama hosted the Columbus (Ohio) Crew professional soccer team as a congratulatory gesture for the team's 2008 Major League Soccer (MLS) championship. The team (seen in Figure 1.1a) presented the president with a soccer ball. Excitedly, on his way back to the Oval Office, Obama tossed the ball in the air and headed it deftly, thereby demonstrating his soccer physics skills and proving that soccer presides in the executive branch. This delighted the press corps that gathered to cover the team visit. *The Dayton Daily News*/Associated Press clipping below tells the story aptly. This example proves that soccer is, indeed, on the rise in the United States.

DaytonDailyNews.com/sports

Tuesday, July 14, 2009 | **Page B5**

Crew meet No. 1 fan

President Barack Obama on Monday, July 13, welcomed the Columbus Crew to the White House to congratulate the team on its MLS championship. The President joked that he's been watching plenty of soccer these days – for his daughters' games. He says he's learned two main rules for youth soccer: no matter the position, players should run toward the ball all at once; and snacks at the halftime must never be forgotten. Associated Press photo

Figure 1.1a: Columbus Crew soccer team at the White House
Reprinted with permission of *The Dayton Daily News*

Figure 1.1b: President Obama in action, heading the soccer ball given to him by the Columbus Crew (from: http://columbus.crew.mlsnet.com/gallery/photogallery.jsp?pathid=200907145870518&vkey=t102)

The Physical Versus the Intellectual

"Sure, my body can't do what it did when I was twenty, but I've learned so much over the years about being a smart competitor that I have a leg up when I race younger athletes."

> —Dara Grace Torres, American swimmer who won three silver medals at the 2008 Beijing Olympics at the age of forty-one

There is always the physical aspect of soccer, but there also exists the intellectual aspect. This book is intended to train young soccer players not to rely solely on the physical aspects. One can gain tremendous competitive advantage by coupling intellectual know-how with the conventional physical skills of the game. The quote by Dara Grace Torres above confirms the author's own concept of the "novice swimmer syndrome," whereby the novice swimmer expends much more effort and energy than a skilled swimmer, who takes advantage of fluid dynamics effortlessly and swims more efficiently. Playing soccer efficiently implies getting better results with respect to the level of effort applied. Efficiency is formally defined as the ratio of output (result) to input (effort) according to the equation below:

$$e = \frac{output(\text{result})}{input(\text{effort})}$$

The better one understands soccer intellectually, the higher the efficiency of playing the game. In effect, the physics behind the game of soccer helps us to understand the game better and makes it possible to play the game more efficiently.

Soccer can be more fun if and when the player plays a mental game with himself and against the opponent to gain an advantage. In his playing days, the author didn't always run as fast as he could if he didn't need to. To him, a sun-cast silhouette of an opponent offered almost as much information as direct visual contact. For example, when playing forward with the sun to his back, he used the length of the shadows of the defenders chasing him to assess how close they were. He then used that information to change his speed and direction. This, of course, comes with split-second assessment and decision making, which follows years of intellectual dedication.

He also did just-in-time assessment of opponents' height, speed, and "volume" to determine how best to beat them in the air or on the ground. *Volume* is a comical term he used on the field to convey the overall size of an opponent. His philosophical utterances before, during, and after games not only conveyed intellectual underpinnings of the game, but also provided comic relief to teammates, thereby creating an overall more fun experience for everyone. As a coach, he would often shout instructions to his players by saying, "Impossible angle, impossible angle," which meant that whatever the player was trying to do was not possible within the realm of field geometry and physical possibility. Later, he would chastise a failed attempt with "You should have known that, judging the speed and direction of the ball, that movement could not have been executed successfully."

Linking Soccer to STEM

The Physics of Soccer: Using Math and Science to Improve Your Game is unique and targeted because it proactively links the sport of soccer to STEM. Physics, in particular, is the vehicle of choice to communicate that linkage. STEM facilitates an intellectual advantage not only in the workplace but also on the playing field. Through this book, the author has transferred his lifelong interest in soccer into an educational tool that is fun and easy to encourage youths to think and act scientifically, whether playing sports or engaging in another passion. The primary audience for the book is adolescents who are in a position to appreciate physics fully; however, the book can also serve as a head start for sub-adolescents to get an early introduction to the beauty of science as applied to sports.

The English soccer player David Beckham achieved worldwide acclaim for his skill at scoring goals from free kicks by "bending" or curving the soccer ball toward the goal. Such directional mastery of the ball's path, no doubt, has underlying principles of physics, manifested through routine execution after many years of practice. The time span of repeated practice can be shortened through more scientific embodiment of the shooting process.

The purpose of this book is not to provide an exhaustive introduction to physics, but rather to whet the appetite of the adolescent soccer player enough to seek more in-depth pursuit of the interesting subject matter of STEM in general, and physics in particular. STEM is a pathway for advancement for the present and for the future. This chapter presents a brief introduction to each of the elements of STEM before initiating the focus on physics and soccer in the next chapter. Although the primary audience for the book is adolescents, younger kids can also benefit from the early introduction to the principles of STEM. Studies have shown that children under the age of six are capable of learning multiple languages. As early as possible, the brain gets wired for multiple lanes of language reasoning. So, why not get them to start learning the language of STEM earlier on? In other words, children can learn to "speak" math and science very early in their lives. Coupling the learning experience with the fun of sports participation makes the overall process much more effective.

Science

Science[12] (from the Latin word *scientia*, meaning "knowledge") refers to any systematic knowledge or practice. In its more usual interpretation, science refers to a system of acquiring knowledge based on scientific method, as well as to the organized body of knowledge gained through such research. Science consists of two major categories:

- Experimental science
- Applied science

Experimental science is based on experiments (Latin: *ex-periri*, "to try out") as a method of investigating causal relationships among variables and factors. Applied science is the application of scientific research to specific human needs. Experimental science and applied science are often interconnected. Science is the effort to discover and increase human understanding of how the real world works. Its focus is on reality that is independent of religious, political, cultural,

---

12.   http://en.wikipedia.org/wiki/Science

or philosophical preferences. Using controlled methods, scientists collect data in the form of observations, record observable physical evidence of natural phenomena, and analyze the information to construct theoretical explanations of how things work.

Knowledge in science is gained through research. The methods of scientific research include the generation of conjectures (hypotheses) about how something works. Experiments are conducted to test these hypotheses under controlled conditions. The outcome of this empirical scientific process is the formulation of a theory that describes human understanding of physical processes and predicts what to expect in certain situations.

A broader and more modern definition of science includes the natural sciences, along with the *social* and *behavioral sciences*, as the main subdivisions. This involves the observation, identification, description, experimental investigation, and theoretical explanation of phenomena. The social and behavioral aspects of team-based soccer make it particularly amenable to the application of science in its broad sense.

Technology

A strict definition of technology is quite elusive. But in its basic form, it relates to how humans develop and use tools. Knowledge and use of tools and crafts constitute the application of knowledge. *Technology* is a term with origins in the Greek word *technologia*, formed from *techne* ("craft") and *logia* ("saying"). Technology can refer to material objects of use by the society, such as machines, hardware, or utensils. It can also encompass broad areas covering systems, methods of organization, and techniques. The term can be applied generally or to specific areas of application, including the following:

- Communication technology (e.g., cell phones)
- Construction technology (e.g., super highways)
- Medical technology (e.g., X-ray imaging)
- Weapons technology (e.g., guns)

The origin of humans' use of technology dates back to the conversion of natural resources into simple tools (e.g., stones to arrow heads). The prehistorical discovery of the ability to control fire increased the available sources of food. The invention of the wheel helped humans travel long distances. The development of the roof enabled humans to control their environment. Recent technological advances, including computers, wireless interfaces, and the Internet, have minimized physical barriers to communication and allowed humans to interact on a global scale. The capability of technology often advances on a geometric scale. For example, we have war-fighting technology moving from prehistoric weapons (clubs) to the modern weapons (nuclear bombs). Technology has facilitated more advanced economies that benefit the entire society, such as the emerging global economy. Technology has made it possible for us to participate in more leisure time and assume better working conditions.

Engineering

Engineering is the body of knowledge that focuses on the techniques of designing and building products. It involves applying technical information, scientific knowledge, mathematical principles, natural laws, and physical resources to design and develop materials, structures, machines, devices, systems, and processes that achieve specific application objectives. Even in cases of incomplete or imprecise data, the process of engineering can still be carried out using fuzzy and artificial neural network techniques (Badiru and Cheung 2002). Engineering dates back thousands of years, and it has shaped the origin of modern human development. Archeological evidence exists that a rudimentary practice of engineering took place even in prehistoric times. The common characteristics of engineers through the centuries have been an interest in exploratory engagements and intellectual curiosity about how to build things, both physical and conceptual. Engineering enquiry uses an inquisitive framework that can be expressed in terms of the following equation:

$$Enquiry = W^5 H,$$

where the elements represent the following questions:

- What
- Who
- Where
- Why
- When
- How

Because of its wide applications, engineering is very diverse and ubiquitous in human endeavors. The major branches of engineering offer a variety of career fields and options, including the following:

- Aerospace engineering
- Astronautical engineering
- Agricultural engineering
- Architectural engineering
- Bio-medical engineering
- Ceramic engineering
- Chemical engineering
- Civil engineering
- Electrical engineering
- Geological engineering
- Industrial engineering
- Marine engineering
- Materials engineering
- Mechanical engineering
- Metallurgical engineering
- Mining engineering
- Nuclear engineering
- Petroleum engineering

Mathematics

Mathematics is the foundation for applying science, technology, and engineering to solve problems. It is the study of quantity, structure, space, change, and related topics of pattern and form. Mathematicians seek out patterns, whether found in numbers, space, natural science, computers, imaginary abstractions, or elsewhere. Mathematicians formulate new conjectures and establish their truth by precise deduction from axioms and definitions that are chosen based on the prevailing problem. The most common branches of mathematics for everyday application are the following:

- Algebra
- Calculus
- Geometry
- Trigonometry
- Differential equations

Algebra is the mathematics of quantities (known and unknown). Calculus is the mathematics of variations (i.e., changes in variables). Geometry is the mathematics of size, shape, and relative position of figures and with properties of space. Trigonometry is the mathematics of triangles and their angles (interior and exterior). It is the study of how the sides and angles of a triangle relate to one another. Differential equation is a mathematical equation for an unknown function of one or several variables that relates the values of the function itself and its derivatives of various orders. Differential equations play a prominent role in engineering, physics, economics, and other disciplines.

A practical example of the application of differential equations is the modeling of the acceleration of an object (e.g., a soccer ball) falling through the air considering only gravity and air resistance (Bender 2000). Through the effect of gravity, as depicted in Figure 1.2, everything that goes up must come down eventually (Hewitt 1999), unless it escapes the Earth's atmosphere. The flight path of a soccer ball is a parabola[13] plus air resistance and spin. The ball becomes significantly nonspherical after each bounce, which, along with spin and air resistance, causes the curvilinear path to deviate slightly from the expected perfect parabola. With a skillful use of this physics principle, a player can put a bend on the ball when it is kicked à la "bend it like Beckham" soccer fame.[14]

---

13. http://en.wikipedia.org/wiki/Parabola
14. www.hollyscoop.com/david-beckham-pictures/96.

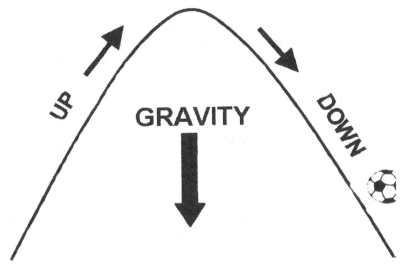

Figure 1.2: Up, gravity, and down flight path of a ball

Gravity-Assisted Versus Gravity-Impeded

The acceleration of a ball toward the ground is the acceleration due to gravity minus the deceleration due to air resistance. Gravity is a constant, but air resistance is proportional to the ball's velocity. This means that the ball's acceleration is dependent on its velocity. An object falling toward the ground is gravity-assisted, while an object going up in the air is gravity-impeded. Consider the case of running uphill versus running downhill. Obviously, you would prefer the gravity-assisted path. Because acceleration is the derivative of velocity, solving this type of motion problem requires the mathematical technique of differential equations.

Speed, Velocity, and Acceleration

At this point, it is important to distinguish between speed and velocity. A complete soccer player needs to be fast, quick, and agile. Being fast (i.e., speedy) means having the ability to cover much distance quickly. Being quick means having the ability to change one's direction or speed very rapidly. This essentially means acceleration. Speed is a scalar.

Scalars are quantities with only magnitude. The direction does not matter. If you are traveling on the interstate at 120 km/hour south or 120 km/hour north, your speed is still 120 km/hour, regardless of whether it is northward or southward. **Speed conveys the rate of change of distance per unit time regardless of direction.** Other examples of scalar quantities are suit size, mass, area, and energy.

Velocity is a vector. Both direction and quantity must be stated. If one plane has a velocity of 560 km/hour north, and a second plane has a velocity of 560 km/hour south, the two planes have different velocities, even though the magnitude of their speed is the same. Figure 1.3 illustrates the velocity of a plane. Other examples of vectors are force and field intensity. Speed is a scalar; velocity is a vector. Based on the foregoing discussion, the reader can now better appreciate the relationships between a player's mass, agility, and ability to exhibit collision avoidance during a game.

Velocity: Magnitude and direction

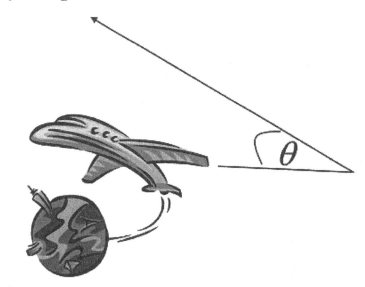

Figure 1.3: Magnitude and direction of a vector

Both speed and velocity are important for playing soccer. Moving objects don't always travel with erratic and changing speeds, but in soccer they do, depending on the tempo of the game and directional changes of ball possession. Normally, an object will move at a steady rate with a constant speed. That is, the object will cover the same distance every regular interval of time. For instance, a marathon runner might be running with a constant speed of 6 meters per second (m/s) in a straight line for several minutes. If the speed is constant, then the distance traveled every second is the same. The runner would cover a distance of six meters every second. If we could measure the runner's position (distance from an arbitrary starting point) each second, then we would note that the position would be changing by six meters each second. This would be in contrast to an object that is changing its speed. An object with a changing speed would be moving a different distance each second. This is exactly what happens during a game of soccer. Speed is a player's ability to outrun opponents, while quickness (acceleration) is the ability to outmaneuver opponents. To complement speed and acceleration, a player must also be agile, which is the ability to adapt to new situations in a game swiftly and effortlessly.

It is essential for young soccer players to possess a basic knowledge of science, technology, and mathematics in order to avoid the pitfall depicted in Figure 1.4, illustrated by the author.

Figure 1.4: STEM lecture on soccer

Widespread Impact of STEM

One of the purposes of this book is not only to explain the physical phenomenon of the game of soccer, but also to get soccer-playing youths interested in the subject of physics as an area of study. This can help advance interest in STEM initiatives beyond just sports interests. Physics has a wide range of applications in the society (Hafemeister 2007), and science has unique applications to sports for young people (Barr 1990).

Chapter 1 References

Adair, Robert K., *The Physics of Baseball*, HarperCollins, New York, 2002.

Badiru, Adedeji B. and John Cheung, *Fuzzy Engineering Expert Systems with Neural Network Applications*, John Wiley & Sons, New York, NY, 2002.

Badiru, Adedeji B., *STEP Project Management: Guide for Science, Technology, and Engineering Projects*, Taylor & Francis/CRC Press, Boca Raton, FL, 2009.

Barr, George, *Sports Science for Young People,* Dover Publications, New York, NY, 1990.

Bender, Edward A., *An Introduction to Mathematical Modeling*, Dover Publications, Mineola, NY, 2000.

Daish, C. B., *The Physics of Ball Games*, English University Press, London, 1972.

Gay, Timothy, *The Physics of Football*, HarperCollins, New York, NY, 2004.

Hafemeister, David, *Physics of Societal Issues: Calculations on National Security, Environment, and Energy*, Springer, New York, NY, 2007.

Halliday, David, Robert Resnick, and Jearl Walker, *Fundamentals of Physics Extended*, 7th ed., Wiley, Hoboken, NJ, 2007.

Hewitt, Paul G., *Conceptual Physics*, 3rd ed., Addison-Wesley, Longman, CA, 1999.

Hopp, Wallace J. and Mark L. Spearman, *Factory Physics,* 3rd ed., McGraw-Hill International Edition, McGraw-Hill/Irwin, Boston, MA, 2008.

Chapter 2
Physics and Motion

"Intellectual growth should commence at birth and cease only at death."

—Albert Einstein

Albert Einstein's Contributions

Everything we do is predicated on motion of one form or another. Physics is essential for motion. It's through physics that we reach out into space, as shown in the opening graphic for this chapter. Albert Einstein,[15] the scientist who developed the most famous physics equation in history, said, "Intellectual growth should commence at birth and cease only at death." This quote encourages continual learning about the world around us. Curiosity does not kill the cat; it makes the cat wiser. A better understanding of the applications of physics in our everyday lives provides an avenue for the intellectual growth that the quote urges us to embrace. The many contributions of Albert Einstein's work are still seen in many of our science and technology products of today. The youths of today, who will become the scientists of tomorrow, can benefit a great deal from the continual learning model espoused by Albert Einstein.

Definition of Physics

Physics, derived from the Greek word *physis*[16] (meaning "nature"), is the natural science that explains fundamental concepts of mass, charge, matter, and its motion, as well as all properties that arise from the concepts, such as energy, force, space, and time. Physics is the general analysis of nature, conducted in order to understand how the physical world behaves. Physics is a major player (pun intended) in STEM, and it deserves a special treatment and understanding. Principles of physics are embedded in or complemented by several other scientific bodies of knowledge such as astronomy, chemistry, mathematics, and biology. Because of this symbiotic relationship, the boundaries of physics remain difficult to distinguish. Physics is

15.   http://en.wikipedia.org/wiki/Albert_einstein
16.   www.absoluteastronomy.com/topics/Physics

significant and influential because it provides an understanding of things that we see, observe, and use every day such as televisions, computers, cars, household appliances, and sports. The game of soccer, in particular, is subject to many of the principles of physics.

Wide Applications of Physics

Physics covers a wide range of phenomena of nature, from the smallest (e.g., subatomic particles) to the largest (e.g., galaxies). Included in these phenomena are the very basic objects from which all other things develop. It is because of this that physics is sometimes said to be the "fundamental science." Physics helps to describe the various phenomena that occur in nature in terms of easier-to-understand phenomena. Thus, physics aims to link the things we see around us to their origins or root causes. It then tries to link the root causes together in an attempt to find an ultimate reason for why nature is the way it is.

As examples, the ancient Chinese observed[17] that certain rocks (e.g., lodestone) were attracted to one another by some invisible force. This effect was later called magnetism and was first rigorously studied in the seventeenth century. A little earlier than the Chinese, the ancient Greeks knew of other objects, such as amber, that when rubbed with fur, would cause a similar invisible attraction between the two. This was also first studied rigorously in the seventeenth century and came to be called electricity. Thus, physics had come to understand two observations of nature in terms of some root cause (electricity and magnetism). However, further work in the nineteenth century revealed that these two forces were just two different aspects of one force: electromagnetism. This process of unifying or linking forces of nature continues today in contemporary studies of physics.

Major Branches of Physics

The major branches of physics are shown in Figure 2.1, which shows different size/speed combinations of matter (Cutnell and Johnson 2006, Giancoli 2004, Halliday et al. 2007, Kuhn 1996).

17. www.scribd.com/doc/17312254/Physics

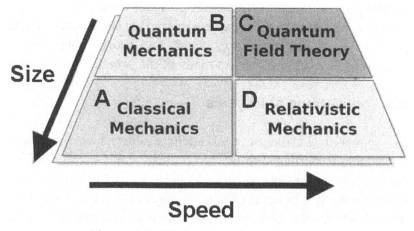

Figure 2.1: Major branches of physics

Branch A: Classical mechanics. This deals with matter of large size and slow speed. Size is of huge order (e.g., ranging up to planetary sizes) while speed is of small order (e.g., race bike speed).

Branch B: Quantum mechanics. This deals with matter of small size and slow speed. Size is of around subatomic order, while speed is comparable to that of a race bike.

Branch C: Quantum field theory. This branch deals with matter of small size and large speed. Size is of around subatomic order, while speed is of large order, comparable to the speed of light.

Branch D: Relativistic mechanics. This deals with matter of large size and large speed. Size is of the order ranging up to planetary sizes, while speed is of large order, comparable to the speed of light.

Scientific Conversion Factors

Scientific notation and conversion factors are important for the application of STEM to our day-to-day activities, including sports. This section presents the most common conversion factors. It is essential that methods of evaluating measured data be understood so that quantities can be assessed and appreciated properly. As an illustration,[18] in late September 1999 the **National Aeronautics and**

---

18. www.cnn.com/TECH/space/9909/30/mars.metric/, accessed

Space Administration's (NASA's) $125 million Mars orbiter crashed onto the surface of Mars because a Lockheed Martin engineering team used English units of measurement while the agency's team used the more conventional metric system for a key operation of the spacecraft. The mismatch prevented navigation information from being transferred between the spacecraft team at Lockheed Martin in Denver and the flight team at NASA's Jet Propulsion Laboratory in Pasadena, California. A summary of metric conversion factors is presented in Figure 2.2. More detailed conversion factors are presented in the Appendix.

September 12, 2009. CNN Web posting, "NASA's metric confusion caused Mars orbiter loss," September 30, 1999.

Condensed Metric Conversion Table

Kilometer-Mile Conversion

Kilometers	Miles		Miles	Kilometers
1	0.62		1	1.61
5	3.11		5	8.05
10	6.21		10	16.09
20	12.43		20	32.19
30	18.64		30	48.28
40	24.86		40	64.37
50	31.07		50	80.47
60	37.28		60	96.56
70	43.50		70	112.65
80	49.71		80	128.75
90	55.92		90	144.84
100	62.14		100	160.93
500	310.69		500	804.67
1,000	621.37		1,000	1,609.34

Metric Tables

Capacity

10 milliliters	= 1 centiliters
10 centiliters	= 1 deciliter
10 deciliters	= 1 liter
10 liters	= 1 dekaliter
10 dekaliters	= 1 hectoliter
1,000 liters	= 1 kiloliter (stone)

Area

100 sq. millimeters	= 1 sq. centimeter
100 sq. centimeters	= 1 sq. decimeter
100 sq. decimeters	= 1 sq. meter
100 sq. meters	= 1 are
10,000 sq. meters	= 1 hectare
100 hectares	= 1 sq. kilometer

Length

10 millimeters	= 1 centimeter (cm)
10 centimeters	= 1 decimeter
10 decimeters	= 1 meter (m)
10 meters	= 1 dekameter
100 meters	= 1 hectometer
1,000 meters	= 1 kilometer (km)

Weight

10 milligrams	= 1 centigram
10 centigrams	= 1 decigram
10 decigrams	= 1 gram
1,000 grams	= 1 kilogram (kilo)
100 kilograms	= 1 quintal
1,000 kilograms	= 1 metric ton

Metric Equivalent of U.S. Weights and Measures

Dry Measure

1 pint =	.550599 liter
1 quart =	1.104197 liters
1 peck =	8.80958 liters
1 bushel =	.35238 hectoliter

Liquid Measure

1 pint =	.473167 liter
1 quart =	.946332 liter
1 gallon =	3.785329 liters

Avoirdupois Measure

1 ounce =	28.349527 grams
1 pound =	.453592 kilogram
1 short ton =	.90718486 metric ton
1 long ton =	1.01604704 metric tons

Long Measure

1 inch =	2.54 centimeters
1 yard =	.914401 meter
1 mile =	1.609347 kilometers

Square Measure

1 sq. inch =	6.4516 sq. centimeters
1 sq. foot =	9.29034 sq. decimeters
1 sq. yard =	.836131 sq. meter
1 acre =	.40469 hectare
1 sq. mile =	2.59 sq. kilometers
1 sq. mile =	259 hectares

Cubic Measure

1 cu. inch =	16.3872 cu. centimeters
1 cu. foot =	.028317 cu. meter
1 cu. yard =	.76456 cu. meter

Figure 2.2: Condensed metric conversion table

Chapter 2 References

Cutnell, John D. and K. W. Johnson, *Physics*, 7th ed., Wiley, Hoboken, NJ, 2006.

Giancoli, Douglas C., *Physics: Principles with Applications*, 6th ed., Pearson Education, Upper Saddle River, NJ 2004.

Halliday, David, Robert Resnick, and Jearl Walker, *Fundamentals of Physics Extended*, 7th ed., Wiley, Hoboken, NJ, 2007.

Kuhn, Karl F., *Basic Physics: A Self-Teaching Guide*, Wiley, Hoboken, NJ, 1996.

Chapter 3
Energy and Work

Physical Science of Energy

Energy is, indeed, a fascinating topic both from an intellectual and usage standpoints. Even if, as engineers, we are already versed in the science of energy, putting the present energy crisis in a social context will be informative. We must understand the inherent scientific characteristics of energy in order to fully appreciate the perilous future that we face if we don't act now. There are two basic forms of energy (Cutnell and Johnson 2006):

- Kinetic energy (KE)
- Potential energy (PE)

All other forms of energy are derived from the above two fundamental forms. Energy that is stored (i.e., not being used) is potential energy. Energy transfer research enables us to understand how energy goes from one form to another.

Kinetic energy is found in anything that is in motion (e.g., waves, electrons, atoms, molecules, and physical objects). Anything that moves produces kinetic energy, but what prompts it to move requires its own source of energy. Electrical energy is the movement of electrical charges. Radiant energy is electromagnetic energy traveling in waves. Radiant energy includes light, X-rays, gamma rays, and radio waves. Solar energy is an example of radiant energy. Motion energy is the movement of objects and substances from one place to another. Wind is an example of motion energy. Thermal or heat energy is the vibration and movement of matter (atoms and molecules inside a substance). Sound is a form of energy that moves in waves through a material. Sound is produced when a force causes an object to vibrate. The perception of sound is the sensing (picking up) of the vibration of an object.

Potential energy represents energy content by virtue of gravitational position as well as stored energy. For example, energy due to fuel, food, and elevation (gravity) represents potential energy. Chemical energy is energy derived from atoms and molecules contained in materials. Petroleum and natural gas are examples of chemical energy. Mechanical energy is the energy stored in a material by the application of force. Compressed springs and stretched rubber bands are examples of stored mechanical energy. Nuclear energy is stored in the nucleus of an atom. Gravitational energy is the energy of position and place. Water retained behind the wall of a dam is a demonstration of gravitational potential energy. Light is a form of energy that travels in waves. The light we see is referred to as visible light. However, there is also an invisible spectrum. Infrared or ultraviolet rays cannot be seen, but can be felt as heat. Sunburn is an example of the effect of ultraviolet energy on the skin. The difference between visible and invisible light is the length of the radiation wave, known as *wavelengths*. Radio waves have the longest rays, while gamma rays have the shortest rays.

In summary, kinetic energy is the energy of moving objects. It depends on an object's mass and velocity.

$$KE = \frac{1}{2}mv^2$$

Where:

m = mass

v = velocity

Potential energy is the energy stored in an object located at a height above the Earth's surface. It depends on how high above the ground the object is positioned.

$$PE = mgh$$

Where:

m = mass

g = gravity

h = height above the ground

For trajectory motion, the potential energy at the top of the trajectory is equal to the kinetic energy at the bottom of the trajectory. The total energy of the trajectory system is kinetic energy plus potential energy.

Work is the transfer of energy through mechanical means. It is the term used to describe how energy changes kinetic energy to potential energy. Work accomplished is equivalent to kinetic energy. It is important to note the following:

- When work is negative, kinetic energy decreases. For example, an upward movement of a soccer ball implies a decrease in KE.
- When work is positive, kinetic energy increases. For example, a downward movement of a soccer ball implies an increase in KE.

Energy Conservation Issues

When we ordinarily talk about conserving energy, we often refer to reducing our consumption in order to save energy. According to Newton's law, energy cannot be created or destroyed. When energy is consumed, it does not disappear; it simply goes from one form to another. For example, solar energy cells change radiant energy into electrical energy. As an automobile engine burns gasoline (a form of chemical energy), it is transformed from the chemical form to a mechanical form. When energy is converted from one form to another, a useful portion of it is always lost, because no conversion process is perfectly efficient. It is the objective of energy engineers to minimize that loss by putting the loss into another useful form. This is why industrial engineers mathematically model the interaction of variables in an energy system in order to optimize energy resources when designing new products.

Harnessing Natural Energy

It is a physical fact that there is abundant energy in the world. Use of the resource is just a matter of meeting technical requirements to convert it into useful and manageable forms from one source to another. For example, every second, the sun converts 600 million tons of hydrogen into 596 million tons of helium through nuclear fusion. The remaining 4 million tons of hydrogen is converted into energy in accordance with Einstein's theory of relativity, which famously states that:

$$E = mc^2,$$

where E represents energy, m represents mass of matter, and c represents speed of light. This equation says that energy and mass are equivalent and transmutable. That is, they are fundamentally the same thing. The equation confirms that a very large amount of energy can be released quickly from an extremely small amount of matter; the *right matter,* for that matter. This is why atomic weapons are so powerful and effective. The theory of relativity is also the basic principle behind the way the sun gives off energy, by converting matter into energy. What the sun produces is a lot of energy that equates to 40,000 watts per square inch on the visible surface of the sun. This can be effectively harnessed for use on Earth, and it accounts for the ongoing push to install more solar systems to meet our energy needs.

Although the Earth receives only a tiny fraction (one half of a billionth) of the sun's energy, there is still a great potential to harness the energy for useful purposes. Comprehensive technical, quantitative, and qualitative analysis is required to harness this energy around the world. Industrial engineering and operations research can play an important role in that energy pursuit. The future of energy will involve several decisions involving technical and managerial issues such as the following:

- Point-of-use generation
- Co-generation systems
- Micro-power generation systems
- Energy supply transitions
- Coordination of energy alternatives
- Global energy competition
- Green-power generation systems
- Integrative harnessing of sun, wind, and water energy sources
- Energy generation, transformation, transmission, distribution, storage, and consumption across global boundaries

- Socially responsible negawatt systems (i.e., to invest in reducing electricity demand instead of investing to increase electricity generation capacity)

All of the above details about energy are important for sports just as they are for all other human pursuits. The more soccer players appreciate these details, the more they will be more socially responsible consumers of energy. Even the minuscule issue of conserving energy while playing has long-term implications in the overall scheme of our existence.

Energy Over Vast Distances

The universe offers tremendous amounts of natural energy, albeit over vast distances. Light, in its various spectra, forms the basis for a lot of the energy in the universe. Light travels fast and across vast distances to bring us life-supporting energy on Earth.

Speed of light $\approx$ 299,792,458 meters per second
$\approx$ 186,000 miles per second
$\approx$ 669,600,000 miles per hour

Speed of sound $\approx$ 340.29 meters per second
$\approx$ 0.211446403 miles per second
$\approx$ 761.207051 miles per hour

Conversion factors are presented in the Appendix. Online reference materials and other published sources provide extensive information about the speed of light. The term *speed of light* refers to the speed of light in a vacuum (i.e., free space). This is a fundamental physical constant usually denoted by the symbol c. It is the speed of all electromagnetic radiation, including visible light. The speed of light in a vacuum is *exactly* 299,792,458 m/s.

A light-year is the distance light travels in one year. Thus, at the speed noted above, one light-year translates to 5,878,499,810,000 miles traveled by light in one year. That is,

$$1 \text{ light-year} = 5.87849981 \times 10^{12} \text{ miles}$$
$$1 \text{ light-year} = 9.4605284 \times 10^{12} \text{ kilometers}$$

Celestial objects that are rated as being so many light-years away represent vast distances travelled by light before we can observe those objects on Earth. In specific cases, celestial lights that we observe on Earth at this point in time actually started traveling from the emitting objects millions of years ago, before reaching us now for present-day observation. Imagine an object in a galaxy that is 50 million light-years away. What we see now occurred 50 million years ago in that galaxy. To put things in perspective, what is happening on a distant star right now won't be observed on Earth for millions of years into the future. The speed of light is a fundamental constant of space and time. No matter or information can travel faster than the speed of light.

For many practical purposes, the speed of light is so great that it can be regarded as instantaneous travel. An exception is where long distances or precise time measurements are involved. For example, in the global positioning system (GPS), a GPS receiver measures its distance to satellites based on how long it takes for a radio signal to arrive from the satellite. In astronomy, distances are often measured in light-years, which is explained above.

It should be noted that the speed of light when it passes through a transparent or translucent material medium, like glass or air, is less than its speed in a vacuum. The speed is inversely proportional to the refractive index of the medium. In specially prepared media, the speed can be very small or even zero. If a projectile or spacecraft is sent upward with an initial speed of 11.2 km/s (25,200 MPH or 7 miles per second), it would leave the Earth. This is called the "escape velocity" from Earth's surface.

In the Blink of an Eye

To put relative speeds into perspective, consider the speed of the blink of an eye. We often hear of comparisons to what happens "in the blink of an eye." For example, cars on a highway race past a mile marker in the blink of an eye, or a fast soccer player zooms by a defender in the blink of an eye. Well, the average blink generally lasts between 300 and 400 milliseconds. That is, three tenths to four tenths of a second. How fast is this on a miles-per-hour scale? This is an interesting exercise left to the calculation and imagination skills of readers. In solving this riddle, consider the distance covered by a blink within its four-tenths-of-a-second speed rating. What about the speed of a wink? After all, a wink could be a form of covert communication among teammates during a soccer game.

Simple Machines for Accomplishing Work

With physics, there are ways of making work easier. The most common tools for accomplishing work fall in the category of six simple machines, which are described in this section. All machines, no matter how large or complex, are made up of combinations of the six simple machines. Although they all may not be directly applicable to the game of soccer, the six simple machines help to emphasize the importance of physics in our everyday activities.

A machine is a tool that enables a force to be applied at a certain point by the application of another force at a different point. Machines are usually designed so that a small effort may overcome a large load. For example, a soccer player may be able to juggle the ball effortlessly, controlling the ball in impossible ways through the application of the principles of simple machines.

The ratio of load to effort is called mechanical advantage (MA). That is, the mechanical advantage is the ratio of the force of resistance to the force of effort. This is represented by the equation below, which is available from various published physics sources (Cutnell and Johnson 2006, Giancoli 2004, Halliday et al. 2007, Kuhn 1996, Ominsky and Harari 1994):

$$MA = \frac{F_R}{F_E}$$

Where:
MA = mechanical advantage

F_R = force of resistance (N)

F_E = force of effort (N)

The mechanical advantage is the factor by which a machine multiplies the force put into it. The efficiency of a machine is given by the ratio of "useful work done by the machine" to the "work done on the machine." That is, efficiency (e) is defined as:

$$e = \frac{\text{work output of a machine}}{\text{work input to the machine}}.$$

A perfect machine has an efficiency of 1. Actual machines have efficiencies much less than 1. Velocity ratio of a machine is the ratio defined as:

$$vr = \frac{\text{distance effort moves}}{\text{distance load moves}},$$

where "distance effort moves" represents the amount of effort applied in a particular direction and "distance load moves" represents how far the subject of the effort moves in a particular direction.

Simple Machine 1: The Lever

A lever consists of a rigid bar that is free to turn on a pivot, which is called a fulcrum. The lever is a bar supported at a single point, the fulcrum. The positioning of the fulcrum changes the mechanical advantage of the lever. For example, by placing the fulcrum at a certain point, we may be able to lift a 200-pound weight with the application of a force of only 100 pounds. In ancient Egypt, builders used the principle of levers to move and position stone pillars weighing more than 100 tons. Greek mathematician Archimedes (*c.* 287 BC to *c.* 212 BC) is reported to have said, "Give me the place to stand, and I shall move the earth." The schematic of a lever is shown in Figure 3.1. The respective distances and forces are represented as D1, D2, F1, and F2, respectively.

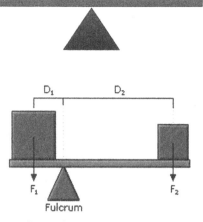

Figure 3.1: Simple machine 1: Lever

When a lever is in static equilibrium (i.e., balanced), the following mathematical relationship holds:

$$\mathbf{F_1 D_1 = F_2 D_2}$$

The effort arm represents where force is input. The effort arm is always larger than the resistance arm. The force applied at end points of the lever is proportional to the ratio of the length of the lever arm measured between the fulcrum and application point of the force applied at each end of the lever. Mathematically, this is expressed by $M = Fd$. There are three classes of levers representing variations in the location of the fulcrum and the input and output forces. They are shown in Figure 3.2, Figure 3.3, and Figure 3.4. The mechanical advantage is also calculated as:

First-Class Levers

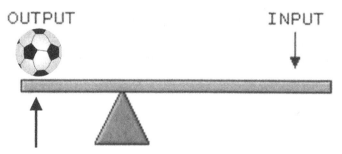

Figure 3.2: First-class levers

Examples:

1. Seesaw (also known as a teeter-totter)

2. Crowbar

3. Pliers (double lever)

4. Scissors (double lever)

5. Flip (e.g., flipping a soccer ball using a rigid bar)

Second-Class Levers

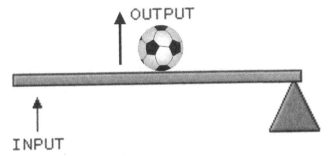

Figure 3.3: Second-class levers

Examples:

1. Wheelbarrow

2. Nutcracker (double lever)

3. The handle of a pair of nail clippers

4. An oar

5. Lift (e.g., balancing a small soccer ball on the instep and raising it by tilting the foot using the heel as the fulcrum)

Third-Class Levers

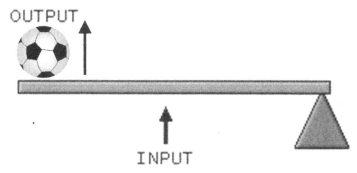

Figure 3.4: Third-class levers

Examples:

1. Human arm

2. Tongs (double lever) (where hinged at one end, the style with a central pivot is first-class)

3. Catapult

4. Any number of tools, such as a hoe or scythe

5. The main body of a pair of nail clippers in which the handle exerts the incoming force

Simple Machine 2: Wheel and Axle

A wheel and axle consists of a large wheel attached to an axle so that both turn together. Any large disk (the wheel) attached to a small-diameter shaft or rod (the axle) can provide mechanical advantage for performing work. Turning a screw with a screwdriver is a simple example of a wheel and axle. The fundamental equation of wheel and axle is presented in Figure 3.5.

$$F_R \times r_R \times = F_E \times r_E \, ,$$

where

F_R = force of resistance (N)

F_E = force of effort (N)

r_R = radius of resistance wheel (m)

r_E = radius of effort wheel (m)

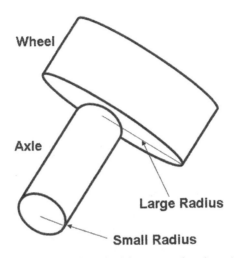

Figure 3.5: Simple machine 2: Wheel and axle

The mechanical advantage for a wheel and axle is represented as shown below:

$$MA_{\text{wheel and axle}} = \frac{r_E}{r_R}$$

This is the ratio of the radius of the wheel to the radius of the axle. If the radius of the wheel is four times greater than the radius of the axle, every time we turn the wheel once, the force applied will be multiplied four times. Examples of wheel and axles include bicycles, Ferris wheels, gears, wrenches, doorknobs, and steering wheels.

Simple Machine 3: The Pulley

A pulley, shown in Figure 3.6, is any rope or cable looped around a support. A very simple pulley system would be a rope thrown over a branch to hoist something into the air. Often, pulleys incorporate a wheel and axle system to reduce the friction on the rope and the support.

Figure 3.6: Simple machine 3: Pulley

If a pulley is fastened to a fixed object, it is called a "fixed pulley." If the pulley is fastened to the resistance to be moved, it is called a "moveable pulley." When one continuous cord is used, the ratio reduces according to the number of strands holding the resistance in the pulley system. The effort force equals the tension in each supporting stand. The mechanical advantage of the pulley is given by the following formula:

$$MA_{\text{pulley}} = \frac{F_R}{F_E} = \frac{nT}{T} = n$$

where
T = tension in each supporting strand
n = number of strands holding the resistance

F_R = force of resistance

F_E = force of effort

Simple Machine 4: The Inclined Plane

An inclined plane (Figure 3.7) is a surface set at an angle from the horizontal and used to raise objects that are too heavy to lift vertically. Often referred to as a *ramp*, the inclined plane allows us to multiply the applied force over a longer distance. In other words, we exert less force but for a longer distance. The same amount of work is done, but it just seems easier because it is spread over time.

Figure 3.7: Simple machine 4: The inclined plane

If an object is put on an inclined plane, it will move if the force of friction is smaller than the combined force of gravity and normal force. If the angle of the inclined plane is 90 degrees (rectangle), the object will free fall. Example of an inclined plane is a ramp. In soccer ball juggling, for example, a skillful player can use his outstretched leg and thigh as a ramp to roll the ball down (as shown below) onto his foot before flipping the ball into a juggling routine. Figure 3.8 shows an illustration of a leg and thigh in an inclined plane posture.

Figure 3.8: Thigh and leg as inclined plane

The mechanical advantage of an inclined plane is:

$$MA_{\text{inclined plane}} = \frac{F_R}{F_E} = \frac{1}{h},$$

where

F_R = force of resistance (N)

F_E = force of effort (N)

l = length of plane (m)

h = height of plane (m)

Simple Machine 5: The Wedge

A wedge works in a similar way to the inclined plane, only it is forced into an object to prevent it from moving or to split it into pieces. A knife is a common use of the wedge. Other examples are axes, forks, nails, and door wedges. The wedge is a modification of the inclined plane. The mechanical advantage of a wedge can be found by dividing the length of either slope by the thickness of the longer end. In the illustration below, the tip of the soccer shoe is used as a wedge to separate the ball from the ground; thereby lifting the ball up for further skillful ball handling. The illustration in Figure 3.9 shows the tip of a soccer shoe used as a wedge.

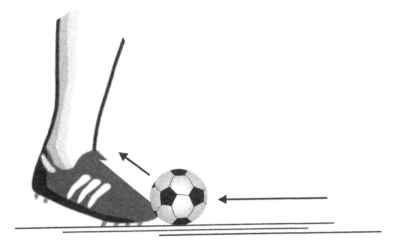

Figure 3.9: Using soccer shoe as a wedge

As with the inclined plane, the mechanical advantage gained by using a wedge requires a corresponding increase in distance. The mechanical advantage is calculated by the expression below:

$$MA = \frac{s}{T},$$

where
MA = mechanical advantage
s = length of either slope (m)
T = thickness of the longer end (m)

Wedges are used as either separating or holding devices. A wedge can be composed of either one or two inclined planes. A double wedge can be thought of as two inclined planes joined together with their surfaces sloping outward.

Simple Machine 6: The Screw

A screw is an inclined plane wrapped around a circle or rod. A screw can be used to move a load (like a corkscrew) or to split and separate an object (like a carpenter's screw). From the law of machines, we have the following equation:

$$F_R \times h = F_E \times U_E$$

For advancing a screw with a screwdriver, the mechanical advantage is given by the equation below:

$$MA_{screw} = \frac{F_R}{F_E} = \frac{U_E}{h} \,,$$

where

$F_R = $ force of resistance (N)

$F_E = $ effort force (N)

$h = $ pitch of screw

$U_E = $ circumference of the handle of the screw

Chapter 3 References

Cutnell, John D. and K. W. Johnson, *Physics*, 7th ed., Wiley, Hoboken, NJ, 2006.

Erdman, Emily and Madelaine Holden, "Physics of a Soccer Kick," Web site accessed August 31, 2009. clackhi.nclack.k12.or.us/physics/projects/Final%20Project-2005/3-FinalProject/soccerBall/Intro%20Page.html

Giancoli, Douglas C., *Physics: Principles with Applications*, 6th ed., Pearson Education, Upper Saddle River, NJ 2004.

Halliday, David, Robert Resnick, and Jearl Walker, *Fundamentals of Physics Extended*, 7th ed., Wiley, Hoboken, NJ, 2007.

Kuhn, Karl F., *Basic Physics: A Self-Teaching Guide*, Wiley, Hoboken, NJ, 1996.

Ominsky, Dave and P. J. Harari, *Soccer Made Simple: A Spectator's Guide*, First Base Sports, Los Angeles, 1994.

Chapter 4
Soccer Basics

"All work and no play makes Jack a dull boy."
"All play and no work makes Jack a mere toy."

—Proverbs

The premise of this book is to use the intersection of soccer field geometry and the principles of physics to present basic approaches to conquering the game of soccer. Figure 4.1 illustrates the two tools of soccer: the foot and the ball.

Figure 4.1: The foot and the ball

Did You Know?

In a ninety-minute game of soccer, on the average, an average player has ball possession for only about three minutes total. Wow! That small? Read on and you will find out later in Chapter 8 how this amount is calculated. This is why a player needs to play intelligently and make the most use of the limited ball possession time.

Historical Accounts of Soccer

The historical accounts of soccer and other background details presented here, comical as some of them are, are culled from various published sources (Ominsky and Harari 1994, Wade 1997, Wesson 2002) as well as online Web sources.[19]

Although many of the accounts are unsubstantiated, they nonetheless offer an entertaining glimpse of the origin and evolution of soccer. The game of soccer, known as football in most parts of the world, has a long and illustrious history.[20] The origin of the game is debatable. It is obvious that the game originated at a time of limited written records; hence, the fuzziness of when the first soccer game took place. Since all humans evolve with the basic instinct of kicking things around, it is the view of this author that soccer-like games evolved gradually and simultaneously in different parts of the world. But soccer, as we know it today, was reportedly first played as a game in England in the mid-nineteenth century. It appears, though, that soccer's origin goes further back. Different countries, groups of people, and individuals have offered opinions, albeit from biased viewpoints, on who invented games involving the use of feet and some object similar to a "ball." The *Fédération Internationale de Football Association* (FIFA) archived an article about the history of soccer that credits the Chinese with inventing the game. The only documented reference to the origin of soccer is from the observations of Greek historian Herodotus of Halicarnassus (fifth century BC), who described a game played by soldiers in which the defeated team captain's head would be severed, dipped in melted rubber, and used for the play of the rematch. The following unsubstantiated claims were culled from various Web sources (authors unknown):

- "It started in Brazil when a few children were playing together when they saw a bucket of soft rubber which came from a rubber plantation nearby. Then, one of them got an idea and turned it into a ball-shape. So, the children played with each other but not in the modern way. They just passed to each other without touching with their hands. Some tourist

---

19. www.all-soccer-info.com/
20. www.soccerballworld.com/History.htm

happened to pass by and saw what had happened and decided to change the game with two goal posts and twenty a side."

- "Soccer was first played as a game by Roman soldiers, who used the heads of their enemies in a game with simple goal posts. So it's understandable why there is a rule against touching the ball with your hands. Just kick it again."
- "It began in Italy with small rocks, we now call Bacchic ball, played by the Roman soldiers when bored at their post, progressed to larger rocks, then due to the difficulty in the weight, material was sewn together to form a large ball. Each century there were modifications made, until today."
- "Soccer came to Europe from the Mexicans; after a battle they would chop off their opponents' heads and use them as football. This form of entertainment was then taken across to Europe by the Spaniards, Portuguese, Dutch, and so on."
- "The historical origin of soccer was in China in about 2600 BC. They used a ball made of leather. The goals were about thirty feet high and twenty feet apart and was played in celebration of the emperor's birthday. The name was called Tsi chu. It was played during the Hun Dynasty."
- "Soccer was invented by the Mayan and Aztec Indians in Central America. At the Mayan ruins, in the city of Copan, Honduras, they had one of the first soccer fields ever. This civilization dates back to more than 10,000 years ago. In this civilization, soccer teams would compete against each other, and the captain of the winning team was sacrificed after the game. The act of being sacrificed was considered an honor to these people."
- From the history of soccer page at About.com: "There is documentary evidence that a game or skill building exercise, involving kicking a ball into a small net, was used by the Chinese military during the Han Dynasty—around the second and third centuries BC. Earlier evidence of a field marked out to play a ball-kicking game has been found at Kyoto, in Japan. Both the Greeks and ancient Romans played a soccer-type game which resembled modern soccer—although in

this early version, teams could consist of up to twenty-seven players!"

- "It is believed that the first recorded soccer game took place on a Shrove Tuesday in Derby, England, as part of a festival to celebrate the victory of English soldiers over Roman troops (AD 217). By 1175 the annual Shrove Tuesday soccer game was a regular event."

- "It is correct that a lot of games were played in the history of mankind where something was kicked around. As well as tennis, volleyball or hacky sack are not simply defined by the fact that a ball is played over a net, soccer is not defined by trying to kick something into whatever goal. The game we know as soccer today was founded in the English public schools in the early nineteenth century by simple school boys that played the game, although it was mostly forbidden. They discussed and changed the rules of the game. Later the games were allowed and seen as good training for manhood and fairness. To give an extra challenge to fair play and self-control, the boys of Eton forbade the use of the hands. As not being allowed to use the hands is the main characteristic of soccer in contrast to rugby, it appears that was the moment when soccer was born. Soccer and rugby parted and went different ways; and the former became the sport we know as soccer today. Soccer later spread to the Continent, where the first national game was Austria against Hungary."

- "Soccer was believed by scientists to have been started in the Chinese Han Dynasty in 1000 BC. They think that it was played by the military to make sure that the soldiers were ready for battle. It was later played in the Roman and Greek civilizations, but with many more players and not that many rules. It is known for a fact that soccer was played in AD 600 in Kyoto, Japan. Later, football was played in the United Kingdom by people of all sorts. The king of England thought that soccer should be banned because of how dangerous it was, but no one could stop soccer because it had become too popular of a sport. Today soccer is all over the world and considered to be the most popular sport of all."

Global Phenomenon

Soccer is a global phenomenon, a national adoration in most countries except the United States. But the United States is gaining fast in the spread, acceptance, and appreciation of the game of soccer. The World Cup, which is held every four years, took place in the United States in 1994. That event helped to boost the visibility and youth participation of soccer throughout the country. The Major League Soccer in the United States has continued to heighten the American consciousness of the game. Worldwide, more people watch soccer than any other sport. Surprisingly, international soccer has been played in the United States longer than in any other country except Britain. Official documentation states that in 1885, the United States and Canada played the first international soccer match outside the British Isles. As the wall hanging in Figure 4.2 shows, Nigeria's participation in the 1994 World Cup in the United States was a source of national pride.

Figure 4.2: Nigeria's Super Eagles at 1994 U.S. World Cup

Physics of Soccer Stampede

Because of its worldwide appeal, soccer often elicits passion and sentiments that can run amuck. Fan and spectator stampede is one major area of concern. Dangerous and tragic stampedes have occurred at many international soccer games, particularly in Europe and South America. The impact of a crushing force applied during a stampede can easily lead to tragedy. The control of soccer crowds, whether at the ticket line or in the spectator stands, should be one of the major concerns of game administrators. The author's pencil drawing in Figure 4.3 illustrates this concern.

Figure 4.3: Soccer game ticket line

Categories of Soccer Abilities

One of the key aspects of engineering is breaking down complex phenomena into their more simple components. Using an engineering rationale, a soccer player's abilities can be broken down into three main categories:

A. Ball Control Skills

> These abilities allow you to make the ball do what you want, whether passing, shooting, or dribbling. These result from repeated practice, depending on your learning curve. They include the following:
> > i.   Passing
> > ii. Trapping
> > iii. Dribbling
> > iv. Shooting

B. Mobility Skills

These abilities get you to where you want to be on the field before your opponent does. They are often innate, god-given abilities, but sometimes still trainable. They include the following:

    i. Speed

    ii. Acceleration

    iii. Agility/coordination and change of direction

    iv. Stamina

C. Intelligence

This involves knowing the best method to achieve an objective. This results from experience, instruction, and mental preparation. It includes the following:

    i. Communication, leadership, and team chemistry

    ii. Strategy and tactics

    iii. Anticipation, action, reaction, and preemption

    iv. Vision: ability to see and draw inferences from game situations

The Physics of Soccer: Using Math and Science to Improve Your Game covers all the above categories of abilities. Happy reading!

Basics of the Game

- The object of the game is to put the ball in the net with any part of the body except the hands and arms.
- In a standard game format, each team starts with eleven players, from a roster that can be as large as twenty-two players (that means eleven starters and eleven reserves). In some countries, these are called the *first eleven* and the *second eleven*.

- Each team is allowed to substitute the goalkeeper (called *goalie* in the United States) and two other players.
- Each goal counts as one point.
- Each game consists of two forty-five-minute halves with no timeouts.
- The referee keeps the official time and adds "injury time" at the end of each half to compensate for play stoppages.

The game of soccer is such that it can be extremely difficult to score goals. Many soccer games end in 0-0 ties or 1-0 victories. This fact has led to several popular soccer jokes such as the following:

- "Soccer players do it for ninety minutes without scoring."
- "Male soccer players make a pass, but do not score, in coed games."

The author himself added this original quote to the soccer lexicon:
"Scoring in soccer is as hard as pulling a tooth and threading it through the eye of a needle."

Constraints and Opportunities

The constraints to which the modern game of soccer is subjected create opportunities to be creative and innovative with physics-based motion analysis. The difficulty in scoring in a soccer game necessitates developing ingenious ball movement strategies to set up scoring opportunities. Skills thus learned can become a lifelong asset in tackling other challenges of life.

Soccer Equipment

Soccer is, perhaps, the easiest major sport to get into. Soccer players can be outfitted inexpensively, which is why it is very popular with schools and adored by parents. Soccer requires only three basic pieces of equipment: the ball, soccer shoes, and shin guards. In fact, in many parts of the world, players dispense with the shin guards as they engage in "bare-knuckles" games. With the basic equipment accomplished, all that soccer players need is an open field or space, which doesn't even have to meet regulation standards. Thus, neighborhood kids in many parts of the world turn any open space, whether dirt, grass, or paved, into a soccer playing field.

The Ball

The soccer ball is a spherical (round) object preferably made of leather. In developing countries, soccer balls may be made from cheap plastic-based materials. Standard soccer ball sizes are tabulated in Table 4.1. Ball specifications are usually presented by age or levels of play (competition).

Table 4.1: Soccer ball sizes and specifications

Size	Circumference (Inches)	Weight	Age
5	27–28	14 oz.–16 oz.	12 and up
4	25–26	11 oz.–13 oz.	8–11 years
3	23–24	11 oz.–12 oz.	7 and under

In the old days of full-leather uncoated soccer balls, a ball could get soggy and heavy (beyond regulations) when playing in the rain. Note that the circumference, and hence, the diameter, of the ball is important for the physics and geometry of motion of the ball as presented in this book. Minute changes of the ball's dimension can make a difference between ruling a ball out of bounds or within bounds in fast-paced games. Ball dimensions also impact the geometrical calculation examples and illustrations presented throughout this book.

Soccer Shoes

The preferred way to play soccer is to wear lightweight leather shoes with interchangeable cleats for different field conditions. But poor soccer-playing kids in developing countries manage quite well playing bare-footed on un-grassed, dirt surfaces. In fact, some consider wearing shoes as a hindrance to their ball control abilities.

Shin Guards

Plastic shin guards are often used to protect a player's legs from vicious kicks during soccer games. In safety-conscious cultures, shin guards must be in place before a player is allowed to participate. The shin guard must be rigid enough to provide the desired protection and yet pliable enough to not impede the player's movements.

The Kickoff

Soccer matches start with a kickoff, after a coin toss. The team that wins the coin toss can choose to kick off or select which side of the field to defend. Also, every time a goal is scored, the scored-upon team restarts play with a kickoff. As a field soccer player, you can do anything you want with the ball, except touch it with your hands or arms. Only the goalie is allowed to handle the ball, except when a field player does the throw-in, as described below.

Throw-In

After one team sends the ball out of bounds along the sidelines, the opposing team is awarded a throw-in. A throw-in is taken along the touchline at the point where the ball went out of play. For a throw-in, both feet must touch the ground and ball release must be done with both hands simultaneously. The ball must be thrown into play with both hands, from behind and over the head. The thrower must face the field of play. As he releases the ball, each foot must be on the ground either behind or on the touchline. If these rules are infringed, the opposing team is awarded a throw-in. No goal can be scored from a throw-in, and the thrower may not play the ball again until it has been touched by another player.

Dribbling

Dribbling (shown in Figure 4.4) is, no doubt, the most fascinating skill in soccer. The player kicks and maneuvers the ball deftly down the field as he tries to get by the opposing players. This is one of the areas where the physics of motion (of the player and ball) is most evident.

Figure 4.4: Demonstration of soccer dribbling skill

Heading

In heading the ball (demonstrated in Figure 4.5), the player strikes the ball with his forehead, sometimes twisting the head to spin the ball and put it into a desired directional path. Goals scored with a header are often the most beautiful execution of soccer skills. The player must keep his eyes on the ball at all times. The player must ensure that he strikes the ball rather than allowing the ball to strike him. This allows directional control of the ball as well as the level of hitting force applied.

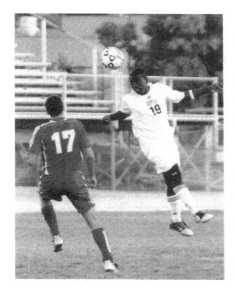

Figure 4.5: Demonstration of soccer heading skill

When heading the ball, a player should make eye contact with the ball before and after striking the ball. When aiming a header, vectors must be taken into account. Under ideal conditions, the angle of incidence equals the angle of reflection. The following computational example is adapted from an online source.[21] A soccer player aims a header downward from 2.00 m above the ground at an angle of 32 degrees (below the horizontal). If the initial velocity of the soccer ball is 8.00 m/s and air resistance is omitted, what is the horizontal distance (along the X-axis) traveled by the ball? The various equations used in projectile motion problems are applicable to this problem. We first determine the components of the initial velocity as follows:

$$\text{X velocity: } V_x = V(\cos\theta)$$
$$\text{Y velocity: } V_y = V(\sin\theta)$$
$$V_{0x} = 8.00 \text{ m/s } (\cos 32°) = 6.78 \text{ m/s}$$
$$V_{0y} = 8.00 \text{ m/s } (\sin 32°) = 4.24 \text{ m/s}$$

We now use the y velocity to calculate the amount of time the soccer ball was in the air. We can set $y = 0$ and $y_0 = 2.00$ to show that we want to know when the ball hit the ground. Note that:

---

21   www.unc.edu/~ncrani/heading.htm

$$Y = y_0 + v_{0y}t + (1/2)a_y t^2$$

That is,

$$Y = 2.00 + 4.24t + (1/2)(-9.8)\ t^2 = 0$$

The −9.8 value represents deceleration due to gravity.

Using the quadratic formula, we obtain $t = 1.20$ s. To find the range travelled by the ball, we can substitute this time value into the equation to find the x position of the ball as follows:

$$X = x_0 + v_{0x}t$$
$$X = 0 + 6.78(1.20) = 8.16 \text{ m}$$

Other relevant computational examples are available in Cutnell and Johnson (2006), Giancoli (2004), Halliday et al. (2007), and Kuhn (1996). Erdman and Holden (2009) posted an online Web video clip of a soccer ball being kicked to generate data for graphing the trajectory of a soccer ball.

Trapping

In trapping the ball, the player brings the ball under control using the foot, thigh, chest, or head. The skill of trapping the ball is an exciting demonstration of the physics of motion, as the player can bring a ball traveling at a high speed to a complete and controllable stop. This then allows the player to move the ball in a different direction.

Passing

In passing the ball (as in Figure 4.6), the player sends the ball to other players on the team with pinpoint accuracy to avoid interception by opposing players. Passing skills often help to demonstrate a player's selflessness and sportsmanship. Passes are executed over both short and long distances. Accuracy and timing are essential for successful passes.

Figure 4.6: Demonstration of soccer passing-on-the-run skill

Playing the Ball

Except at throw-ins, the goalkeeper is the only player allowed to play the ball with his hands or arms, and he does so only within his own penalty area. A field player (as well as the goalie) may use any other part of the body to stop, control, or pass the ball, move with it, or score. The following may be used: feet, head, thigh, chest. These are illustrated in Figure 4.7a. In Figure 4.7b, a player provides actual demonstrations of ball control.

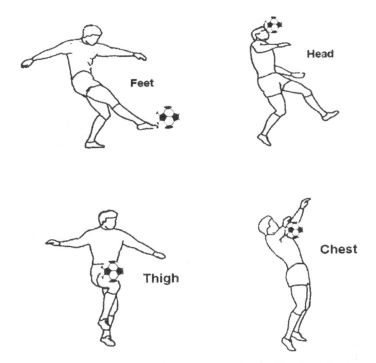

Figure 4.7a: Using body parts for ball control

Figure 4.7b: Player demonstration of ball control moves

Scoring

A goal is scored when the whole of the ball has crossed the goal line under the crossbar and between the goal posts, provided that the attacking team has not infringed the laws. Following a score, play restarts with a kickoff taken by the team against whom the goal is scored.

Goal Kick

A goal kick is awarded to the defending team when the ball crosses their end-line after having been last touched by an opponent. The kick may be taken by any player of the defending side, including the goalkeeper. The ball is placed on the six-yard line within the half of the goal area nearer the point where it crossed the goal line, with the following provisions:

1. The kick must send the ball out of the penalty area.

2. The kicker may not touch the ball again until it has been played by another player. All opponents must retreat outside the penalty area until the kick is made.

3. No goal can be scored directly from a goal kick.

Corner Kick

A corner kick is awarded to the attacking team if the ball crosses the goal line having been last played by the defending team. It is taken from the quarter circle by the corner flag on the appropriate side of the field with the following provisions:

1. The flag must not be moved to help the kicker.

2. Opponents must remain ten yards away until the kick is taken (until the ball has traveled its circumference).

3. A goal can be scored directly from a corner kick but the kicker must not play the ball again until it has been touched by another player.

Free Kick

A free kick is either direct or indirect and is taken from where the offense occurred.

A *direct free kick* is one from which the player taking the kick can score directly.

An *indirect free kick* is one from which a goal cannot be scored until the ball has been touched by another player. At any free kick, all opponents must be ten yards from the ball, except at an indirect free kick less than ten yards from the goal, when they must stand between the goal posts. If the defending side is given a free kick in its own penalty area, no opponents may enter the area until the kick is taken. The ball must be stationary at a free kick, and the kicker may not replay the ball until another player touches it.

Offside

Offside rules are the most complex of all the rules of soccer. Offsides must be called under a very fast pace of play, with only a split second to decide. An attacking player is offside if, when the ball is played, he is nearer the opposing goal than two opponents and the ball, unless one of the following is true: he is in his own half of the field; an opponent was the last player to touch the ball; or he receives the ball directly from a goal kick, a corner kick, or a throw-in, or when the referee drops the ball. Although a player may technically be in an offside position, he is not penalized unless in the opinion of the referee he is interfering with play or with an opponent, or is seeking to gain an advantage by being in an offside position.

Fouls and Misconduct

A direct free kick is awarded for the following intentional fouls (a penalty kick is awarded if the fouls are committed by a defender in his penalty area):

- Tripping
- Holding an opponent with a hand or arm
- Playing the ball with a hand or arm (except for the goalkeeper in his penalty area)
- Kicking or attempting to kick an opponent
- Jumping at an opponent or charging in a violent or dangerous manner

- Charging from behind (unless the opponent is guilty of obstruction)
- Striking or attempting to strike an opponent
- Pushing an opponent with the hand or any part of the arm

An indirect free kick is awarded for the following fouls:

- Dangerous play, such as attempting to play the ball while it is in the goalie's hands
- Charging fairly, as with the shoulder, but when the ball is not within playing distance
- Delay of game
- Intentionally obstructing an opponent while not attempting to play the ball, in order to prevent him from reaching it
- Charging the goalkeeper, unless the goalkeeper is holding the ball, is obstructing an opponent, or has gone outside his goal area
- When a goalkeeper takes more than four steps while holding the ball, throwing it in the air and catching it, or bouncing it, without releasing it to another player, or when he deliberately wastes time in playing the ball
- When a player is offside
- When a player taking a kickoff, throw-in, goal kick, corner kick, free kick, or penalty kick plays the ball a second time before another player has touched it
- Dissenting from the referee's decisions
- Entering or leaving the game without the referee's permission
- After a player is sent off for an offense not specified in the laws; for rude conduct
- Using a teammate to gain height to head the ball

Cautioning and Sending Off

The referee must caution a player if he enters or leaves the game without the referee's permission; continually breaks the laws; shows dissent from any of the referee's decisions; or is guilty of unsportsmanlike conduct.

The referee has the power to send a player off the field for the rest of the game if he commits acts of violence or serious foul play (including spitting); uses foul or abusive language; or continues to break the laws after a caution.

Out of Play

The ball is out of play when it completely crosses the boundaries of the field, or when the game has been stopped by the referee. Play is restarted by a throw-in when the ball has crossed the touchline, or by either a goal kick or a corner kick when it has crossed the goal line.

Penalty Kick

Any offense that incurs a direct free kick is punished by the award of a penalty kick to the opposing team when it is committed by a defending player in his own penalty area. A penalty kick is taken from the penalty spot. All players except the goalkeeper and the player taking the kick must stand outside the penalty area, at least ten yards from the penalty spot. The player taking the kick must play the ball forward, and he may not play it a second time until it has been touched by another player. The goalkeeper must stand on the goal line, without moving his feet, until the ball is kicked. The kick is retaken if the defending team violates a rule and a goal is not scored; the attacking team, with the exception of the kicker, infringes and a goal is scored; or there are infringements by players of both sides. If the kicker breaks the rule, for instance by kicking the ball twice, the defending side is awarded an indirect free kick.

With all these constraints, rules, and guidelines, one might theoretically expect a game to run smoothly—if everyone follows the rules. But rarely are rules followed completely, either intentionally or unintentionally. The expectation is that with proper technical skill development, the need for intentional fouling can be minimized. Using the geometrical layout of the field to their advantage, players should learn to play the game rather than play the foul.

The Field Geometry

The soccer field is rectangular and must be 50 to 100 yards wide and 100 to 130 yards long. Figure 4.8 shows a typical soccer field layout. At either end, there is a goal and a goal area enclosed in the larger penalty area. The posts and crossbar of the goals must be of equal width and of the same width as the goal line. The touchlines and the goal lines are part of the playing area. At each corner of the field is a flag on a post that is at least five feet high and must not have a pointed top. Flags on either side of the center line are optional, but must be set back at least one yard from the touchline. Of course, actual playing field geometry in a particular situation can vary from the standard regulation based on space availability, level of play, league preferences, and age-appropriate field size requirements.

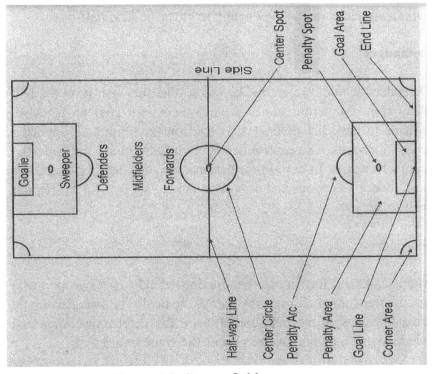

Figure 4.8: Soccer field geometry

Field Positions

Each team puts eleven players on the field. In general terms, midfielders run an average of seven miles during a game. Forwards (strikers) and fullbacks run an average of five miles. Sweepers run an average of four miles. Goalkeepers run an average of two miles during a game. The midfielders are the most mobile of all players and must be in excellent shape to cover all the field areas of their responsibility.

Goalkeepers

Goalkeepers must be very athletic, quick, and good jumpers. They are usually tall, unless their jumping abilities are used to offset height deficiency. They also must be able to both kick and punt the ball downfield at least long enough to cross the field half-line.

Defenders

Defenders should, preferably, be tall so that they can head the ball away from dangerous zones around their own goal areas. Also, it helps to have big defenders to confront or intimidate opposing team's forwards. The central defenders usually guard the opposing team's forwards. In certain formations, the outside wing defenders push forward as wings and provide attacking support for the regular forwards.

Sweepers

Many teams use formations that use one defender as a sweeper, who has the freedom to roam to any part of the field. The sweeper should have full view of the field and strategically determines when and where to move on the field of play as the game progresses.

Midfielders

Midfielders must have good peripheral vision and be able to spot forwards who are free and pass the ball to them. They must have good ball control and the ability to pass the ball accurately. They must be in excellent physical shape to be able to run forward or backward on the field as the game demands.

Forwards

The primary job of soccer forwards is to score goals. They must be nimble, rugged, and skillful. Because of their threat of scoring goals, they are often the targets of rugged and vicious play from opposing players. Forwards usually have tremendous speed so that they can outrun defenders. A forward player must have the instinct to always go for the goal, as shown in Figure 4.9.

Figure 4.9: Beating the goalie on the ground

Because of the range of skills they must possess, forward players are often seen as sensational players. Some of the desired skills of good forwards include shooting (Figure 4.10), jumping to soar above defenders, fast acceleration, fake-away dribbling, outrunning opponents, and superior ball control, as shown in the illustrative photos that follow.

Figure 4.10: Shooting for goal

The Goal Is to Score Goals

In soccer, the ultimate goal is to score a goal (pun intended). You may have a good game, but if you don't score, you don't win. Unlike in many other American sports where various statistics are recorded and used to rank teams and players, soccer's primary assessment tool is the number of goals scored. As shown in the photo below, jumping to soar above opponents to reach for the ball is a desirable skill for all soccer players. Many forwards score goals this way. Defenders protect their teams against threatening goalmouth in-the-air scrambles by their ability to jump and head the ball away. Midfielders control, redirect, and pass the ball with deft high-flying headers. Forwards sometimes have to soar above opponents to score goals, as can be seen in Figure 4.11.

Figure 4.11: Beating the goalie in the air

Rapid Acceleration

Moving from zero (idle speed) to a desired speed to beat an opponent becomes easier if the player is already in motion. The same principle that is advertised for cars in moving from zero to sixty miles per hour, for example, is the same principle that applies to moving from a standing stance to full playing speed. Coaches must train their players to use the principles of physics to build initial motion needed to skip to high speed. The way the game of soccer develops during play, the ball can come from any direction at any time. The ability to react quickly and take advantage of the ball requires proper starting motion and good acceleration. This is demonstrated in Figure 4.12.

Figure 4.12: Beating the defender on the run

Constant Movement Required

"Life is like riding a bicycle. In order to keep your balance, you must keep moving."

—Albert Einstein

Good soccer players must continue to move during a game. In a game of soccer, a player must keep moving in order to secure and maintain an edge over the opponents. Figure 4.13 illustrates the importance of moving and maintaining balance.

Figure 4.13: Bicycle motion and balance

Bringing the Ball under Control

Bringing the ball under control requires directional flexibility of the player. Again, understanding the principles of motion of the ball in relation to the player's motion is a key element of gaining proper control of the ball. Instep and outstep ball control are needed to bring the ball under control effectively. Figure 4.14 shows a demonstration of bringing the ball under control. Once the ball is under control, fast-paced dribbling may ensue, as shown in Figure 4.15.

Figure 4.14: Demonstration of ball control skill

Figure 4.15: Dribbling on the run

Fake-Away Ball Control

Fake-away means sending the ball off in a direction that the opponent cannot easily anticipate. Shifting or switching the ball from one direction to the other keeps opponents guessing and confused about where the ball is going next. In Figure 4.16, the dribbler first faked to the right, then to the left, then back to the right before taking a shot down the field. The more unpredictable the ball direction is, the more fake-away ball control can be executed. For teammates to be in synch, each one must be prepared and ready to receive the ball when it comes. Only the opponents need to be confused ... not teammates.

Figure 4.16: Fake-away ball control

On-the-Run Ball Control

Controlling the ball on the run requires exceptional application of the principles of physics to build speed, change speed, straddle the ball, fake stop, and change directions. Figure 4.17 demonstrates on-the-run ball possession.

Figure 4.17: On-the-run ball control

Straddle-and-Dribble Ball Control

The more a player can shelter the ball away from opponents, the better. Straddling the ball (as shown in Figure 4.18) protects it against an "invading" opponent. Of course, this requires good ball control and deft agility to move the ball in split-second increments.

Figure 4.18: Straddle and dribble ball control

Keeping Eyes on the Ball

The eyes always have it in soccer. A player must keep his eyes on the ball at all times, even when the ball is in the possession of an opponent or teammate. This way, the player can better anticipate what may happen next. A player must have good (or corrected) vision in order to make an accurate assessment of an object's size, geometry, and distance. Players who repeatedly and narrowly miss shots and passes should have their eyes checked. Figure 4.19 illustrates eyeing the ball even while running down the field and scanning the field for the next move.

Figure 4.19: Eyeing the ball while running

Physics of the Human Eye

There is a lot of physics associated with the human eye and the process of vision.[22] A normal and healthy human eye has the ability to adjust itself easily to objects at varying distances. It has a natural "stop" for protecting itself against light of too great intensity. The eye has a convex lens made up of tough crystalline (gelatinous) material. The lens forms an image of the object being viewed on the screen of the eye, known as the retina, at the back of the eye. The most light-sensitive spot on the retina is called the yellow spot. The light impulses are conveyed through here to the brain by the optic nerve and give rise to the sense of vision. The optic nerve is the second of twelve paired cranial nerves, considered part of the central nervous system. Although the image is inverted on the retina, the brain interprets the image as that of an upright object. The top covering of the front of the eyeball, called the cornea, bulges in front of the pupil. The thickened portion of the cornea is responsible for the greater part of the refraction of light entering the eye. Figure 4.20 illustrates the human eye.[23]

22.   www.tedmontgomery.com/the_eye/
23.   webvision.med.utah.edu/anatomy.html

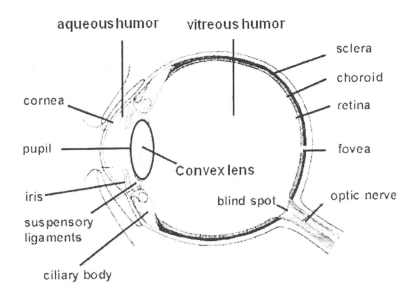

aqueous humor   vitreous humor

sclera

choroid

retina

cornea

pupil

fovea

Convex lens

iris

blind spot

optic nerve

suspensory
ligaments

ciliary body

Figure 4.20: Seeing soccer: physics of the human eye

The cornea, together with the fluid behind it, the crystalline lens, and the clear gel (vitreous humor) behind that, constitute a complex lens system. The ability of the ciliary muscles to alter the focal length of the lens enables the eye to adjust itself to objects at different distances. This is known as the power of accommodation of the eye. The pupil is a hole in the middle of the iris (or colored diaphragm) and appears black because little or no light is reflected from it. If the amount of light received by the eye is great, the pupil in front of the lens contracts and reduces the amount of light entering the eye. If the amount received by the eye is small, the pupil expands (i.e., dilates). The distance between the lens and the retina is fixed and cannot be adjusted for focusing on objects at varying distances. Focusing is accomplished by a ring of muscles surrounding the lens, which can alter the focal length of the lens.

When a distant object is viewed, such as a soccer ball at the other end of the field, the ciliary muscles are relaxed and the eye is said to be unaccommodated. For a normal eye, the focal length of the lens when the eye is unaccommodated is equal to the distance between the retina and eye lens. When the eye is focused on an object at a finite distance from it, the ciliary muscles are tense and the eye is said to be accommodated. Most people cannot observe an object without strain if the object is closer than twenty-five centimeters (or ten inches). This distance is known as the least distance of distinct vision. The point which is a distance of twenty-five centimeters from the eye is known as its near point. The far point of a normal eye is at infinity.

Vision Defects and Correction

Good vision is needed for good soccer. Poor vision should be corrected in order to gain the most from soccer. Common eye defects that soccer players should be wary of include the following:

1. Short-sightedness (myopia)

2. Long-sightedness (hypermetropia)

3. Astigmatism

4. Presbyopia

1. Short-Sightedness (myopia): In some cases, due to a long eyeball, parallel light is brought to a focus at a point in front of the retina. A distant object cannot be clearly seen. This defect is known as short-sightedness. The farthest point from the eye which cannot be focused on the retina is known as the person's far point. This defect can be compensated for by a concave lens.

2. Long-Sightedness (hypermetropia): Long-sightedness is caused by short eyeballs. Due to this defect, a player's eye may not be able to focus effectively on near objects. In this case, the least distance of distinct vision will not be equal to twenty-five centimeters but greater than twenty-five centimeters. A convex lens in front of the eye can correct this defect.

3. Astigmatism: This is an optical defect in which vision is blurred due to the inability of the optics of the eye to focus an object into a sharp image on the retina. This may be due to an irregular curvature (not perfectly round shape) of the cornea and lens. There are two types of astigmatism: regular and irregular. Irregular

astigmatism is often caused by a corneal scar or scattering in the crystalline lens and cannot be corrected by standard lenses. Irregular astigmatism of the cornea can be corrected by contact lenses. Regular astigmatism arising from either the cornea or crystalline lens can be corrected by a toric contact lens, which has two different powers or curvatures so that it can correct for both astigmatism and either myopia (near-sightedness) or hypermetropia (far-sightedness). Toric contact lenses typically combine the effects of a cylindrical lens with those of a spherical lens.

4. Presbyopia: Due to old age when the eye lens becomes inelastic, people are unable to see distant objects, whereby parallel rays converge to a point behind the retina. By accommodating, they are able to bring them to a focus on the retina and, thus, see distant objects clearly. They cannot, however, accommodate sufficiently to see near objects clearly. Presbyopia is corrected by using a suitable convex lens.

Sight and Sound in Soccer

With an understanding of the comparative speeds of light and sound, we can better appreciate their influence in a game of soccer. Because light travels much faster than sound, you see sooner than you hear when the source is far away. Consider the case of seeing lightning before hearing the associated thunder. When the target and the source are close together, it appears that both light and sound arrive at the same time. But that is not the case. Sound is definitely slower, but it has the advantage of not requiring a "line of hearing" as is the case with the "line of sight" in seeing and assessing game situations. The anatomy of the human ear[24] is shown in Figure 4.21. Without going into the complex science of hearing, we should understand the basic principles of what happens in the auditory process.

---

24. http://en.wikipedia.org/wiki/Ear

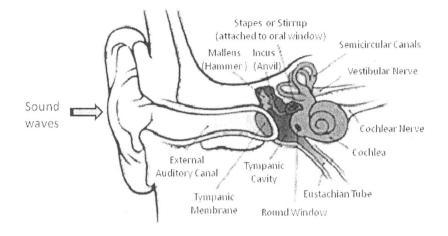

Figure 4.21: Hearing soccer: physics of the human ear

Sound is the sensation that the brain experiences when receptor hairs in the inner part of the ear gyrate back and forth. The inner ear contains hair cells. The microscopic "hairs" of these cells are structural protein filaments that project out into the fluid in the inner ear. The hair cells are mechanical receptors that release a chemical neuro-transmitter when stimulated by sound waves. Sound waves moving through fluid push the filaments. If the filaments bend enough, they cause the hair cells to trigger. In this way, sound waves are transformed into nerve impulses, which the brain receives (i.e., "hears") and interprets.

Sound is a form of energy that moves through air, water, and other matter, in waves of pressure. Sound waves are measured in frequencies in units of hertz (one cycle per second). The human ear can generally hear sounds with frequencies between 20 Hz and 20 kHz (the audio range). For example, in American football, an audible occurs when a quarterback calls out numbers and colors and the offensive players shift into a new formation before a play. This means that the quarterback has changed a play at the line of scrimmage after reading the defense of the other team. Thus, sound is used beneficially in sports for auditory communication. In soccer, the player must listen attentively to any subtle sounds that may indicate the positions and actions of opponents. In Figure 4.22, the dribbler listens for sounds coming from approaching defenders and uses that information to maintain keep-away ball control. In Figure 4.23, the dribbler listens for sounds that he may use to assess how many defenders are converging rapidly on him.

Sound can also be used adversely by opponents and opposing fans for distraction and annoyance to disrupt composure. Soccer stadium noise has been used effectively to make players lose their poise. There have been cases where a player alleges that an opponent said something derogatory to gain an advantage.

Figure 4.22: Keep-away ball control

Figure 4.23: Full-stride dribble

Scanning the Field

Scan the field constantly to monitor what is going on upstream and downstream. General awareness of the field is what makes great players become field marshals of the soccer pitch. Scanning of the soccer field is demonstrated in Figure 4.24.

Figure 4.24: Scanning the field while dribbling

Building Team Chemistry through Training

Aptitude does not come without practice. In addition to individual practice sessions, players must also participate in team training. This helps to hone the skills needed to work as a team during a game. Building team chemistry, both scientifically and figuratively, implies interdependencies of teammates through soccer training (see Figure 4.25). The social and behavioral lessons learned from soccer make each person a better team player, a better individual, and a better partner in life's endeavors.

Figure 4.25: Soccer team practice

Communication during Game

Communication on the field of play can be accomplished through various means. In addition to our normal verbal communication, we can employ all five senses to get information across to teammates. Figure 4.26 illustrates the five senses that can be employed in the communication process. Making eye contact (seeing) is a form of communication. Hearing (listening) is a form of communication. Speaking (verbal) is the common form of communication. Touching (tactile) is a form of communication. Smelling is a form of communication. Even tasting is a form of communication, though rarely applicable in any soccer game scenario. Soccer players should use any of the above senses as much as possible to communicate with teammates during play. In fact, developing nonverbal communication schemes could be a covert approach to communicate with teammates without the opponent sensing what is going on.

For example, using secret team hand signals could be an effective weapon of communication against opponents. In defensive formations against free kicks, *stenosis of the defense line* can be achieved through subtle gestures and jersey pull-in among the defenders. Stenosis is derived from the Greek word meaning, "narrowing of a normally larger opening." It is often used in a medical context, but we use it here to describe closing of gaps in the defensive lineup.

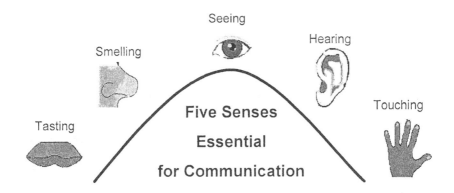

Figure 4.26: Essential senses for soccer communication

Understanding Referees

Frankly, no one seems able to understand referees. They have their ways, and no matter what they do, they are always the butt of jokes and criticism. A referee is in charge of the match. He enforces rules, maintains order, keeps score, and acts as timekeeper. All these responsibilities require tremendous coordination, good physical shape, and impervious response to audience taunts and complaints. Because emotions can run high on the part of players, spectators, fans, coaches, managers, and parents, the job of a referee can be a hazardous one, indeed. There have, in fact, been cases of harm being inflicted upon referees.

Linesmen

Two linesmen (or lineswomen) work with the referee. One linesperson is positioned on each side of the field, covering the length of the field.

They signal the referee if he is unable to see a play. Linespersons use flags to draw the referee's attention. The referee can overrule the linespersons. Linespersons often graduate or move up to become referees.

Yellow Card

When a referee shows a player a yellow card, it represents a caution, which is given for the following:

- Excessive fouling
- Dissent
- Unsportsmanlike conduct

Two consecutive yellow cards in the same game amount to a red card.

Red Card

When a referee shows a player a red card, it represents ejection from the game for the following reasons:

- Violent conduct
- Hard tackling from behind
- Using foul language
- Given a second yellow card

A player who has received a red card is automatically banned from playing in the next game of the team.

Referee and Linesman Signals

Standard referee and linesperson signals[25] shown in Figures 4.27, 4.28, 4.29, 4.30, 4.31, 4.32, 4.33, and 4.34 are adapted from online Web sources.[26]

25. www.firstbasesports.com/soccer_signals.html
26. www.kindersleysoccer.com/Referee%20Signals

Indirect free kick

Advantage – play on

Direct free kick (points in direction of kick)

Figure 4.27: Referee signals image set 1

 Caution (yellow card)

 Sending off (red card)

 Penalty kick (points to penalty kick marker)

Figure 4.28: Referee signals image set 2

 Corner kick

 Goal kick

Figure 4.29: Referee signals image set 3

Figure 4.30: Linesman signals image set 1

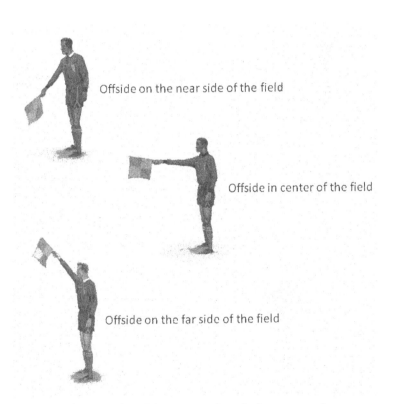

Offside on the near side of the field

Offside in center of the field

Offside on the far side of the field

Figure 4.31: Linesman signals image set 2

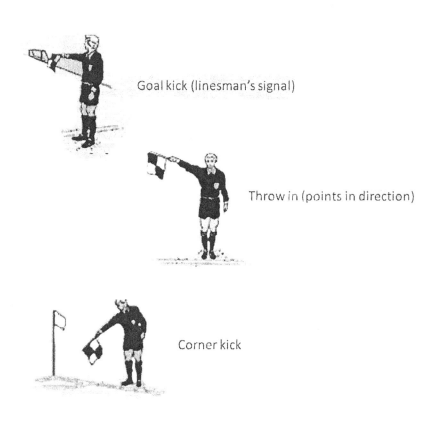

Figure 4.32: Linesman signals image set 3

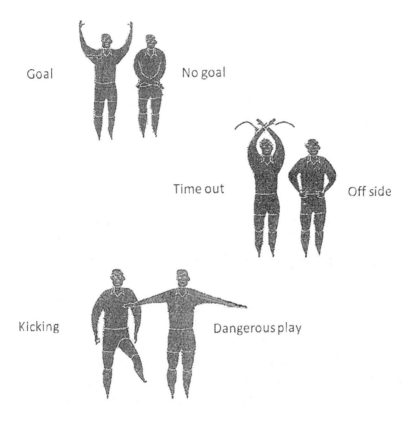

Figure 4.33: General signals image set 1

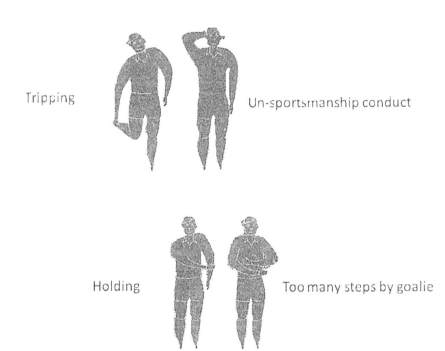

Tripping

Un-sportsmanship conduct

Holding

Too many steps by goalie

Figure 4.34: General signals image set 2

The Joy of Soccer Victory

When it is all said and done and the game plan is executed perfectly, soccer offers a great opportunity for the joy of victory and avoiding the agony of defeat. Kids rejoice in winning, as shown in Figure 4.35. They should be given the opportunity to excel at soccer so they can experience that feeling for real. Figure 4.36 and Figure 4.37 exhibit examples of the spoils of sports victory. Applause, applause, awards, awards!

Figure 4.35: Soccer victory celebration

Figure 4.36: Soccer awards display 1

Figure 4.37: Soccer awards display 2

Starting Young

The key to having a successful lifelong affair with soccer is to start young and make the commitment to continue to enjoy the game through the various stages over the years. The initial stage would normally involve playing in a youth soccer league. The final stage of the soccer love affair may be nothing more than being an avid spectator or a fan. In Figure 4.38, young players strike poses of confidence. Figure 4.39 proves that soccer skills learned in youth, for example, fake-away dribbling, can still be evident in adult playing years.

Figure 4.38: Images of starting young with soccer

Figure 4.39: Skills learned in youth are displayed in adulthood

Chapter 4 References

Cutnell, John D. and K. W. Johnson, *Physics*, 7th ed., Wiley, Hoboken, NJ, 2006.

Erdman, Emily and Madelaine Holden, "Physics of a Soccer Kick," Web site accessed August 31, 2009. www.clackhi.nclack.k12.or.us/physics/projects/Final%20Project-2005/3-FinalProject/soccerBall/Intro%20Page.html

Giancoli, Douglas C., *Physics: Principles with Applications*, 6th ed., Pearson Education, Upper Saddle River, NJ, 2004.

Halliday, David, Robert Resnick, and Jearl Walker, *Fundamentals of Physics Extended*, 7th ed., Wiley, Hoboken, NJ, 2007.

Kuhn, Karl F., *Basic Physics: A Self-Teaching Guide*, Wiley, Hoboken, NJ, 1996.

Ominsky, Dave and P. J. Harari, *Soccer Made Simple: A Spectator's Guide*, First Base Sports, Los Angeles, CA, 1994.

Wade, Allen, *Positional Play: Strikers*, Reedswain Videos and Books, Spring City, PA, 1997.

Wesson, John, *The Science of Soccer*, Taylor & Francis, New York, NY, 2002.

www.unc.edu/~ncrani/heading.htm, accessed September 12, 2009.

www.all-soccer-info.com/, accessed September 12, 2009.

www.soccerballworld.com/History.htm, accessed September 12, 2009.

Chapter 5

Soccer Motion Analysis

Soccer is a game of constant motion. A player must be in shape and be capable of moving at all times while on the field of play. Even without the ball, the movements of a player can still play (pun intended) a significant role in what happens on other parts of the field.

Mechanics and Kinematics

The principles of physics are crucial in understanding the characteristics of a body in motion, be it the soccer ball or a player's body.

Mechanics deals with the relations of force, matter, and motion. This chapter deals with the mathematical methods of describing motion. This computational branch of mechanics is called kinematics. *Motion* is defined as a continuous change of position. In most actual motions, different points in a body move along different paths. The complete motion can be understood if we know how each point in the body moves. We can consider only a moving point in a body or a very small body called a particle. Figure 5.1 shows a generic trajectory of a soccer ball in motion. The position of a particle is specified by its projections onto the three axes of a rectangular coordinate system. As the particle moves along any path in space, its projections move in straight lines along the three axes. The actual motion can be reconstructed from the motions of these three projections.

Biomechanics

Biomechanics is the application of mechanical principles to living organisms. This is particularly important for the practice of sports medicine, where issues of concern include joint instability, design of sports-assistive devices, lower extremity functions, and gait and posture analysis. In effect, biomechanics is a field that combines the disciplines of biology and engineering mechanics and utilizes the tools of physics, mathematics, and engineering to quantitatively describe the properties of biological constituents of living organisms. For example, biomechanics analyzes the internal and external forces acting on the human body (e.g., a soccer player) and the effects produced by the forces.

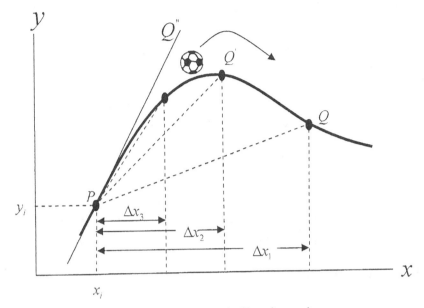

Figure 5.1: Soccer ball trajectories

Average Velocity

If we consider a particle moving along the x-axis, we can plot its x coordinate as a function of time, t. The displacement of a particle as it moves from one point of its path to another is defined as the vector Δx drawn from the first point to the second point. Thus, the vector from P to Q, of magnitude $x_2 - x_1 = \Delta x$, is the displacement. The *average velocity* of the particle is then defined as the ratio of the displacement to the time interval $t_2 - t_1 = \Delta t$. We can represent average velocity by the equation below:

$$\bar{v} = \frac{\Delta x}{\Delta t}.$$

The purpose here is not to overwhelm the reader with intricate details of kinematics; but rather to pique the interest of young readers in understanding that there is some scientific principle behind what happens on the soccer playing field. More advanced readers can consult regular physics textbooks to get the computational details at whatever level they desire (Sears et al. 1977, Serway 1990, Weast 1979, Arfken 1970).

Newton's First Law of Motion

Sir Isaac Newton, a seventeenth-century scientist, developed laws to explain why objects move or don't move. These are known as Newton's laws of motion (Giancoli 2004). Newton's first law of motion, also known as the law of inertia, says the following:

> An object at rest tends to stay at rest and an object in motion tends to stay in motion with the same speed and in the same direction unless acted upon by an unbalanced force (Halliday et al. 2007).

Bring on the Force

What is a force? A **force** is a directional push or pull upon an object resulting from the object's **interaction** with another object. Force is that which changes or tends to change the state of rest or uniform motion of an object. Whenever there is an **interaction** between two objects, there is a force upon each of them. When the **interaction** ceases, the two objects no longer experience the force. Forces exist as a result of an interaction between objects. There are two broad categories of force:

1. Contact force

2. Action-at-a-distance force

Contact forces result from physical contact (interaction) between two objects. Examples include the following:

- Frictional force
- Tensional force

- Normal force
- Air resistance force
- Spring force
- Applied force

Action-at-a-distance forces result even when two interacting objects are not in physical contact with each other, but are still able to exert a push or pull on each other. Examples include the following:

- Gravitational force
- Electrical force
- Magnetic force

Force is a quantity that is measured using the standard metric unit known as the *newton* **(N)**. One newton is the amount of force required to give a 1-kilogram mass an acceleration of 1 m/s/s. Thus, the following unit equivalency can be stated:

$$1 \text{ Newton} = 1 \text{ kg} \frac{m}{s^2}$$

A force is a vector quantity. A vector is a quantity that has both magnitude and direction. To fully describe the force acting upon an object, we must describe both the magnitude (size or numerical value) and the direction.

Newton's Second Law of Motion

Newton's second law of motion states that the acceleration of an object as produced by a net force is directly proportional to the magnitude of the net force, in the same direction as the net force, and inversely proportional to the mass of the object. This law is expressed by the following equation:

$$F = ma,$$

where F is the net force acting on the object. This equation sets the net force equal to the product of the mass times the acceleration.

Acceleration (a) is the rate of change of velocity (v), and velocity is the rate of change of distance.

Newton's first law of motion predicts the behavior of objects for which all existing forces are balanced. The first law states that if the forces acting upon an object are balanced, then the acceleration of that object will be 0 m/s/s. Objects at **equilibrium** (i.e., forces are balanced) will not accelerate. An object is said to be in equilibrium when the resultant force acting on it is 0. For three forces to be in equilibrium, the resultant of any two of the forces must be equal and opposite to the third force. According to Newton, an object will accelerate only if there is a net or unbalanced force acting upon it. The presence of an unbalanced force on an object will accelerate it, thus changing its speed, its direction, or both.

By comparison, Newton's second law of motion pertains to the behavior of objects for which all existing forces are *not* balanced. The second law states that the acceleration of an object is dependent upon two variables: the net force acting upon the object and the mass of the object. The acceleration of an object depends directly upon the net force acting upon the object, and inversely upon the mass of the object. As the force acting upon an object is increased, the acceleration of the object is increased. As the mass of an object is increased, the acceleration of the object is decreased.

Newton's Third Law of Motion

Newton's third law of motion states that **for every action, there is an equal and opposite reaction.** A force is a push or a pull upon an object that results from its interaction with another object. Forces result from interactions between objects. According to Newton, whenever objects A and B interact with each other, they exert forces upon each other. When a soccer player sits in a chair, his body exerts a downward force on the chair, and the chair exerts an upward force on his body. There are two forces resulting from this interaction: a force on the chair and a force on the body. These two forces are called *action* and *reaction* forces in Newton's third law of motion. One key thing to remember is that inanimate objects, such as walls, can push and pull back on an object, such as a soccer ball.

Force Duration and Motion

The longer a force acts on an object, the faster the object will move. When kicking a soccer ball, the longer the foot stays in contact with the ball, the faster the ball will move. This is called "follow-through." It makes the force act longer on the ball to make it go faster. It is common to see good players in golf and tennis continue their swings as long as possible. Similarly, good baseball batters take long swings. Other examples include hammer throwers in track, who swing around several times before letting go, and javelin throwers, who hold on as long as possible by making a complete about-face before releasing the javelin.

Ball Slowdown by Force Duration in Reverse

The principle of *force duration* is applied in reverse when a force slows down an object. The longer a force acts on an object to slow it down, the more effective and smoother the stopping effect. Thus, when a good soccer player receives a fast pass, the ball is brought under control more effectively by elongating the duration of the stopping force. This is accomplished by drawing the foot back as the ball makes contact with the foot. This technique increases the time that the slowing-down force acts on the ball. This way, the ball does not strike the foot with too much sudden impact. This approach lessens the possibility of the ball ricocheting off uncontrollably. When this is executed very well, the ball control is a thing of beauty to watch.

The best display of reverse force-duration skill witnessed by the author was by a high school player at Saint Finbarr's College in Nigeria in 1972. A high ball was descending on the field of play. The player jumped up vertically and connected with the ball about six feet above the ground. As gravity pulled the player back toward the ground, he and the ball came down at the same speed, with the ball resting still on top of his foot. They both reached the ground together, whence he smoothly put the ball back into play on the ground. In many years of playing and watching soccer, the author has never seen any other comparable display of ball stopping skill for a vertically descending soccer ball. The illustration in Figure 5.2 shows how the aerial ball collection is accomplished.

Figure 5.2: Bringing an aerial ball under control

Force Action and Reaction

Shoulder-to-shoulder outmuscling an opponent is allowed in soccer (see Figure 5.3). To accomplish this, a player must build strength to apply force in accordance with Newton's laws of motion. What happens in this case is force application (action) in one direction that is countered by a reaction (push back) in the other direction. If one force exceeds the other, both bodies move in the direction of the higher force.

Figure 5.3: Force action and reaction: shoulder-to-shoulder contest

Centripetal and Centrifugal Forces

Two types of forces that are of interest are centripetal and centrifugal forces. Centripetal force is in effect when an object is in circular motion. Any motion in a curved path involves a force that tends to pull the object toward the center of curvature of the path. *Centripetal* force means "center-seeking" force. The force has the magnitude expressed as shown below:

$$\mathbf{F}_{CP} = m\frac{v^2}{r}$$

Where:
m = mass of the object
v = velocity of the object
r = radius of the circle making up the curved path
v^2/r represents the centripetal acceleration

From the above equation, the centripetal force is proportional to the square of the velocity. This means that a doubling of speed will require four times the centripetal force to keep the object moving on a circular path. If the centripetal force must be provided by friction alone on a curve, an increase in speed could lead to an unexpected skid if friction is insufficient. This explains why a car can skid tangentially off the road when speeding through a curve. Similarly, a mass swinging circularly on a string requires tension in the string. The mass will travel off in a tangential straight line if the string breaks.

Centrifugal force is the converse of centripetal force, as it represents a force that tends to move an object away from the center of its circular path. *Centrifugal* force is a "center-avoiding" force; it is derived from Latin *centrum* ("center") and *fugere* ("to flee"). Objects in a circular rotational frame appear to be under the influence of an outwardly radial force that is proportional to the distance from the axis of rotation and to the rate of rotation of the frame.

Centrifugal force supposedly arises due to the inherent property of mass (also known as inertia), but many physicists do not consider it as a real force. For the purpose of our soccer scientific reasoning here, we will accept it as an imaginary force. Inertia represents the reluctance of a body to change either its speed or direction. According to Newton's laws of motion, a body that is at rest will stay at rest until some force makes it move, and then it will continue to move at the same speed and in the same direction until some force makes it move differently. We may mistakenly think that centrifugal force is what makes an object on a turning car's dashboard slide in a direction opposite the curved path of the car. But the real reason[27] the object slides on the car's dash is because it wants to remain in a straight line (Newton's first law) while the car is turning. This same reasoning is why a little kid may have fun on a school bus sliding on the seat, if there is no restraining seat belt, as the bus goes around sharp turns while the body wants to go in a straight path.

With respect to forces that act on a speeding object, the reader is given the following challenge assignment to be researched and discussed with family members, friends, or classmates:

What makes a speeding car go airborne in an accident?

---

27. Donna Mullenax, technical editorial review comment (September 24, 2009)

Mass and Weight

The mass of an object is an inherent property of the object that conveys the amount of matter contained in the object. Mass is a fundamental property that is hard to define in terms of something else. Any physical quantities can be defined in terms of mass, length, and time. Mass is normally considered to be an unchanging property of an object. The usual symbol for mass is m, and its SI unit is the kilogram. The weight (w) of an object is the force of gravity on the object and may be defined as the mass times the acceleration of gravity (g), as shown below:

$$w = mg$$

Since the weight is a force, its SI unit is the newton. Density is defined as:

$$\text{Density} = \frac{\text{Mass}}{\text{Volume}}$$

Curving the Ball: The Banana Kick

David Beckham is reputed to be able to bend (curve) the ball to throw off defenders and the goalie. The process of curving the ball, well known as the banana kick, uses many of the principles of physics. Execution of the kick is both an art and science. The science part of the execution involves wind speed and direction. The art of it is being able to accurately judge the prevailing environmental conditions and adapt the kick to take advantage of those conditions. While the science of wind shear can be taught, what is even more important are innate good judgment and dedicated practice sessions. That is why some players can execute this kick while others cannot. In order to achieve a banana kick, the ball is not kicked along the line of the center but rather across the ball with a twisting flick of the foot. The result is a spin on the ball that sends the ball on a trajectory often difficult for opponents to guess or defend. Bending of the ball is illustrated in Figure 5.4.

Figure 5.4: Demonstration of ball path into goal

Pressure and Ball Spin Principles

Spinning is of great interest and importance in ball-based sports such as soccer, baseball, tennis, table tennis, volleyball, golf, billiards, and cricket. Complex physics occurs whenever a ball spins. Forces act on the ball in all directions. When all forces are perfectly balanced, the ball is stationary. Superiority of a force in one direction causes motion in that direction. The Magnus effect is normally used to explain the movements of spinning balls. There are three general forces that act on the flight of a soccer ball:

1. Gravity

2. Drag

3. Magnus force

Figure 5.5 illustrates the physics behind the spin. The Magnus force can be described in terms of an imbalance in the drag forces on a ball. The force was known about for centuries, but it was formally described in 1852 by the German physicist, Heinrich Magnus. Earlier, in 1742, a British artillery engineer, Benjamin Robins, had explained deviations in the trajectories of musket balls in terms of this effect.

The schematic below demonstrates the Magnus force acting on a spinning ball. Lines *V* represent the soccer ball's velocity, and the upward arrow represents the resulting force toward the side of the ball with the least pressure. The arrows in the opposite direction to the ball's velocity represent the opposing force due to wind resistance.

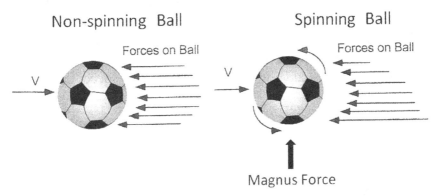

Figure 5.5: Ball spin forces

Impact of Pressure Difference

The effect of pressure difference accounts for many phenomena that we observe or experience. For example, when you drink a liquid with a straw, you create a low pressure inside the straw by sucking air out of it toward the inside of your mouth. The lower pressure (vacuum) created inside the straw forces the liquid, which is under a higher ambient pressure, up the straw and into your mouth. If, when the liquid is halfway up the straw, you block the end of the straw with your tongue, the liquid stays up inside the straw. This is because blocking the straw creates a balance of pressure on either side of the liquid. This causes it to become stationary.

When a ball is spinning in the air, it creates a boundary layer around itself, and the boundary layer induces a more widespread circular motion of the air. If the body is moving through the air with a velocity V, the velocity of the air close to the ball is a little greater than V on one side, and a little less than V on the other. This is because the induced velocity due to the boundary layer surrounding the spinning ball is added to V on one side, and subtracted from V on the other. In accordance with Bernoulli's principle, the velocity is greater when the wind pressure is less; and where the velocity is less, the wind pressure is greater. This pressure gradient results in a net force on the ball and creates subsequent motion in a direction perpendicular to the relative velocity vector (i.e., the velocity of the ball relative to the air flow).

The mathematical theorem called the Kutta-Joukowski theorem[28] relates the lift generated by a right cylinder to the speed of the cylinder through a fluid or air, the density of the fluid or air, and the circulation of the fluid or air. The equation below calculates the lift force generated by inducing physical rotation on a soccer ball.

$$F = \frac{1}{2}\rho\, wrVAl$$

Where:
F = lift force
ρ = density of the fluid
w = angular velocity
r = radius of the soccer ball
V = velocity of the soccer ball
A = cross-sectional area of the soccer ball
l = lift coefficient

The lift coefficient may be determined from plots of experimental data. The spin ratio of the ball is defined by the equation below:

$$\text{Spin ratio} = \frac{(Angular\ velocity)(Diameter)}{2(Linear\ velocity)}$$

For a smooth ball with a spin ratio of 0.5 to 4.5, typical lift coefficients range from 0.2 to 0.6.

---

28. hyperphysics.phy-astr.gsu.edu/HBASE/fluids/kutta.html; en.wikipedia.org/wiki/Kutta%E2%80%93Joukowski_theorem; everything2.com/title/Kutta-Joukowski+lift+theorem

Chapter 5 References

Arfken, George, *Mathematical Methods for Physicists*, 2nd ed., Academic Press, New York, NY, 1970.

Cutnell, John D. and K. W. Johnson, *Physics*, 7th ed., Wiley, Hoboken, NJ, 2006.

Erdman, Emily and Madelaine Holden, "Physics of a Soccer Kick," Web site accessed August 31, 2009. www.clackhi.nclack.k12.or.us/physics/projects/Final%20Project-2005/3-FinalProject/soccerBall/Intro%20Page.html

Giancoli, Douglas C., *Physics: Principles with Applications*, 6th ed., Pearson Education, Upper Saddle River, NJ, 2004.

Halliday, David, Robert Resnick, and Jearl Walker, *Fundamentals of Physics Extended*, 7th ed., Wiley, Hoboken, NJ, 2007.

Kuhn, Karl F., *Basic Physics: A Self-Teaching Guide*, Wiley, Hoboken, NJ, 1996.

Ominsky, Dave and P. J. Harari, *Soccer Made Simple: A Spectator's Guide,* First Base Sports, Los Angeles, CA, 1994.

Sears, Francis W., Mark W. Zemansky, and Hugh D. Young, *College Physics*, 4th ed., Addison-Wesley, Menlo Park, CA, 1977.

Serway, Raymond A., *Physics for Scientists & Engineers*, 3rd ed., Saunders, Philadelphia, PA, 1990.

Wade, Allen, *Positional Play: Strikers*, Reedswain Videos and Books, Spring City, PA, 1997.

Weast, Robert C. (Ed.), *Handbook of Chemistry and Physics*, CRC Press, Boca Raton, FL, 1979.

Wesson, John, *The Science of Soccer*, Taylor & Francis, New York, NY, 2002.

www.all-soccer-info.com/, accessed September 12, 2009.

www.soccerballworld.com/History.htm, accessed September 12, 2009.

www.unc.edu/~ncrani/heading.htm, accessed September 12, 2009.

Chapter 6

Soccer Field Generalship

"Many a trip continues long after movement in time and space have ceased."

—John Steinbeck (1902–1968)

During his playing days, the author was a decent player, not because of his ball-handling skills, but rather because he used every physical aspect of the playing field intelligently. Such practices as proper location, movement, and anticipation of ball directions can help make an ordinary player better. As a player, the author exhibited an uncanny ability to guess an opponent's impossible angle and, thereby, conclude what the opponent could or could not accomplish. He could determine when he should not expend energy needlessly in pursuit of an opponent or the ball. That conservation of energy was then put to other productive uses on the field of play. As the quote opening this chapter shows, strategic positioning on the soccer field can influence how subsequent plays develop. In other words, running into an open segment of the field, even after the movement has stopped, may continue to inspire teammates or discourage opponents about what to do next.

The author has always agonized over the sight of young soccer players who foolishly lurch, jump, or haul themselves after a ball that, in all certainty, is headed across the sideline. If scientific knowledge and physics principles are coupled with ball-handling skills, we can quickly end up with a "lethal" weapon of a soccer player on the soccer-playing pitch. The ability to estimate distance, forecast an opponent's limits of movement, anticipate ball placement, and guesstimate possible versus impossible angles makes players perform at superior levels.

Field Situation Awareness

Every player must be fully aware of the game situation that is evolving and materializing, whether in his immediate environment or down the field. Questions to assess include the following:

- Who has the ball?

- Where on the field is the ball located?
- What direction is the play going?
- Who is in the immediate vicinity?
- When is the game ending?
- How is the weather (wind, sun, heat, cold, etc.)?
- Which team has the edge?

Field Formations and Positional Dynamics

Field formation is an important part of achieving superior soccer field generalship. The author grew up playing the very conventional and classical offensive-minded formation of 2-3-5 (back-middle-forward), which consists of two fullbacks, three midfielders, and five forwards. Coaches of that bygone era lived by the cliché of "the best defense is a good offense." Take the game to the opponent, with five forwards, and you would not have to do much home base defense.

The backfield consists of the following:
- Left fullback
- Right fullback

The middle consists of the following:
- Left halfback
- Center halfback
- Right halfback

The forward batch in the 2-3-5 formation consists of the following:
- Outside left wing
- Inside left forward
- Center forward
- Inside right forward
- Outside right wing

In recent years, formations have evolved into all kinds of strategic positioning. The most popular soccer formations nowadays are 4-4-2 and 4-5-1 for back-middle-forward lineups. These are defensive-minded formations. In the 4-5-1 team formation, the positions are arranged as follows:

Defense: The defenders are normally arranged as outside left, inside left, inside right, and outside right. A common implementation of the formation is to have them lined up in a banana shape with the middle of the curve closest to the goalkeeper and the outside defenders, the points, slightly ahead but behind the midfielders.

Midfield: Two outside and wing players who dominate the flanks of the field. They also act as attackers, creating many scoring opportunities for their teammates. These are hard-working players and must be in excellent shape. This type of positional play cannot be defended by a player-on-player team defense. It requires a good zone defense and constant communication among team members. The inside players are usually defensive in their roles but will become part of the attack when their team has possession of the soccer ball. They will generally use the central midfielder to create plays and control the tempo of the game.

Forward: In this team formation, the team is extremely confident of the lone forward striker. The striker in this formation actually acts as a "post-up" player. This means that this striker at times plays with the opposing defense at his back. This player will try and stretch the defense and receive the ball to lay it back to the oncoming teammates to close the space that the striker has created.

Whatever formation is adopted by a team, the philosophy of this author is that the entire field belongs to the team. Whenever an opportunity develops, each player should be ready and able to move into strategic positions to take advantage of the opportunity, particularly if it can lead to a scoring chance. As a coach, the author once experimented, partly in jest, with what he called a "smorgasbord" formation. Not only did it confuse the opponents, it also confused the team. Although everyone had fun with it, it was quickly dropped as a failed experiment. Many schoolyard pick-up soccer games do use a variation of some smorgasbord formation ... just for the fun of it.

Field Triangulation

The use of triangles plays an important role in the game of soccer. Most practice regimens make use of three-person triangle formations to knock the soccer ball around. If used properly, you can throw opponents off balance by constantly shifting triangle patterns of ball movement. Triangulation, which is the process of measuring by using trigonometry, becomes like second nature to top-notch players, and it is essential for keeping opponents running helter-skelter without effective contact with the ball. That is, an effective use of movement in time and space constitutes playing field generalship that keeps opponents wondering what happened. Common triangle formations are illustrated in Figure 6.1.

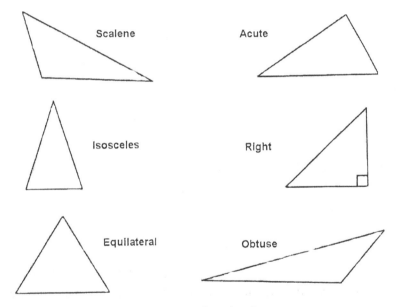

Figure 6.1: Triangle shapes

Scalene Triangle

A scalene triangle with all sides of different lengths; no sides are equal and no angles are equal.

Acute Triangle

An acute triangle is a triangle with its angles less than 90 degrees.

Isosceles Triangle

An isosceles triangle is a triangle with (at least) two equal sides.

Equilateral Triangle

An equilateral triangle is a triangle in which all three sides are equal. Equilateral triangles are also equiangular; that is, all three internal angles are also congruent to each other and are each equal to 60 degrees.

Obtuse Triangle

An obtuse triangle is one where one of the internal angles is greater than 90 degrees.

Right Triangle

A right triangle is a triangle with an angle of 90 degrees. The sides a, b, and c of such a triangle satisfy the Pythagorean theorem, which is represented by the equation below:

$$a^2 + b^2 = c^2,$$

where c (hypotenuse) is the largest side. The other two sides of lengths a and b are called legs, or sometimes _catheti_. An example of triangle formation for ball movement is shown below. Self-initiated lone practice should be used to develop good soccer skills. Just as a coach pushes his team to get better, so should a player push himself or herself to get better. The illustrations in Figure 6.2 and Figure 6.3 show playing the triangles from inside or outside during soccer practice formations where players line up in triangles and trade passing the ball around.

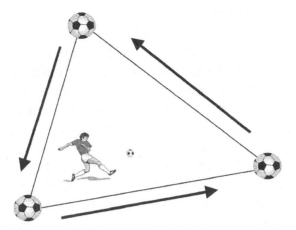

Figure 6.2: Inside triangle ball movement

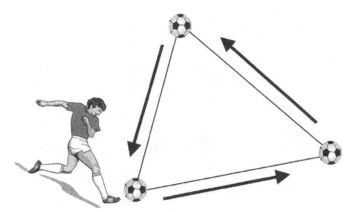

Figure 6.3: Outside triangle ball movement

Geometric Illusions

Trickery and illusion can play a role in sports if one knows how to practice them on the field. What you see is not always what is there. On the soccer field, movement and contrasts can create momentary illusions that confuse what an opponent sees in a flash versus what is actually there. Examples are illustrated in this section. Expert soccer players often use fake movements and illusory trickery to get the ball past opponents.

Completion Figures

Completion figures are figures that the mind interprets momentarily in a particular way despite the fact that the input is incomplete relative to what is typically seen. Illusory contours may be partly accounted for by low-level contrast effects as a mixture of cognitive expectation versus physical and geometric reality. Figure 6.4a illustrates the mind's willingness to see an equilateral triangle and a square despite the fact that there is no information in the picture about the borders for the center triangle or square. A triangle completion illusion makes us see what is not there. The third figure illustrates a soccer ball version of the object border illusion. You will notice that the illusion does not work as well for a soccer ball because we already know cognitively that the ball is spherical and cannot have a "chewed out" segment like in a flat object.

Figure 6.4a: Completion figures set 1

Paradox Illusions

Impossible figures and objects represent paradox illusions that can be used to advantage in geometric formations. Examples of impossible triangles are illustrated in Figure 6.4b. Impossible objects include the impossible stairs and devil's pitchfork, which is a 2-D picture representing a 3-D object (which is not possible).

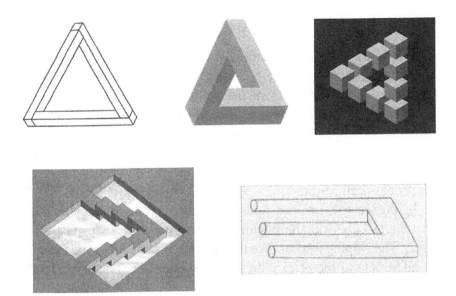

Figure 6.4b: Completion figures set 2

In the famous elephant feet illusion shown in Figure 6.5 (redrawn by author for African tusk size effect), near the ground, we can count five different elephant feet. If we cover up the ground, we can only see four limbs extending from the torso.

Figure 6.5: Illusion of extra elephant foot

Distorting Illusions

Geometric illusions are examples of how the mind attempts to find orderly representations out of ambiguous and disorderly images. The images transmitted from our retina in our eyes to our brain are an imperfect representation of reality (for example, 2-D images cannot accurately represent 3-D space). Our visual system is capable of performing complex processing of information received from the eyes in order to extract meaningful perceptions. Sometimes, however, this process can lead to faulty perceptions or interpretations.

In Figure 6.6, are the lines crooked or straight? If you stare at a single cube, do the adjacent lines appear to slide past each other? The sloping appearance of the lines is created by the vertical misalignment of the black cubes. All the lines are, indeed, perfectly straight and horizontal.

Figure 6.6: Distorting illusion of crooked lines

Some visual stimuli cannot be perceived in a way that agrees with what we can measure physically. Illusions are cases where we find significant differences between perceived and measured reality. In the distortion image shown in Figure 6.7, consider the first two objects. The center connecting line is seen as being shorter in the first figure than in the second figure, but they are actually of the same length. The third object shows both figures superimposed on one another to demonstrate that the center line is of equal length in both of the first two objects. In Figure 6.8, which line segment is longer, AB or BC? They are the same length.

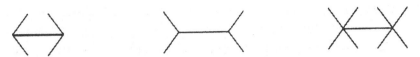

Figure 6.7: Distorting illusion of line lengths

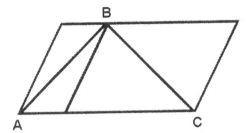

Figure 6.8: Distorting illusion of line lengths

It is easy to perceive one of the middle circles in Figure 6.9 as being smaller than the other. In reality, they are actually of the same size. A soccer ball version of the illusion is also shown.

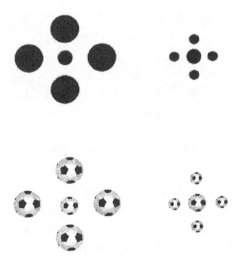

Figure 6.9: Illusion of circle sizes

Perspective, Depth, and Distance

Eyes judge distance based on the size of objects and where the objects are positioned. For example, if you don't know the size of two objects, you may see one as smaller because it is farther away.

In reality, the objects may be of the same size. The picture in Figure 6.10 illustrates this illusion. Perspective is an illusion that makes parallel road lines appear to come together in the distance. Lines that appear to come together in the distance encourage you to have a distorted perception of distance.

Figure 6.10: Perspective over road distance

Geometry of Strides: The Long and Short of It

If you are endowed with shorter limbs, don't even bother to try to outrun long-legged opponents. Instead, try to beat them with other field-generalship strategies. In Figure 6.11, the longer strides will cover more distance per step compared to the average distance. Notice that the strides of a player form a triangle with the ground. An understanding of the shapes, angles, and sizes of triangles help in "sizing up" an opponent and forming an intelligent scientific strategy to outplay the opponent. For example, an intelligent player investigates motion tendencies of opponents and checks out their stability attributes such as center of gravity properties.

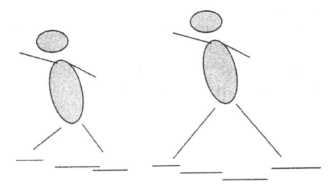

Figure 6.11: Long versus short strides

Extension of Triangles to Mechanics

Distance traveled over a limited time is shown by the area of the trapezoid (i.e., quadrilateral with two parallel sides in the U.S.–based definition) illustrated in Figure 6.12. In the British definition, a trapezoid is a quadrilateral with no parallel sides. Trapezoid and trapezium have exact opposite British and American definitions. The definitions are tabulated in Table 6.1.

Table 6.1: Trapezoid and trapezium definitions

Shape	British definition	American definition
Trapezoid	A quadrilateral with no sides parallel	A quadrilateral with two parallel sides
Trapezium	A quadrilateral with two parallel sides	A quadrilateral with no sides parallel

Properties of a Trapezoid
Base = one of the parallel sides. Every trapezoid has two bases.
Leg = the nonparallel sides are legs. Every trapezoid has two legs.
Altitude = the perpendicular distance from one base to the other. One base may need to be extended to do the calculation or measurement.
Median = a line joining the midpoints of the two legs.
Area = the average base length times altitude.

Perimeter = distance around the trapezoid (i.e., sum of its side lengths). When a soccer coach says "perimeter," he is referring to the distance covered by a certain space.

If both legs of a trapezoid are the same length, this is called an *isosceles trapezoid,* and both base angles are the same. If the legs are parallel, then it has *two* pairs of parallel sides and is a *parallelogram.*

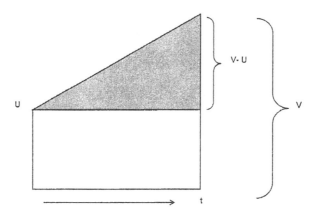

Figure 6.12: Trapezoidal representation of velocities

Calculations based on triangle formations can be used to derive the equations of motion with constant velocity and constant acceleration (Cutnell and Johnson 2006, Giancoli 2004, Halliday et al. 2007, Serway 1990).

Calculating Average Speed and Average Velocity

The average speed during the course of a motion is often computed using the following formula:

$$\text{Average Speed} = \frac{\text{Distance Traveled}}{\text{Time of Travel}}$$

The average velocity is computed using the following equation:

$$\text{Average Velocity} = \frac{\text{Position Displacement}}{\text{Time}}$$

To test understanding of these formulas, consider the following problem: During a ninety-minute game, a soccer player covered a total distance of twelve miles by running and walking around the field. The average speed of the player is calculated as:

$$v = \frac{d}{t} = 12mi / 1.5hr = 8mi / hr$$

Obviously, this is a very busy player with sustainable stamina. The player averaged a speed of 8 miles per hour. He may not have been traveling at a constant speed of 8 MPH. He was undoubtedly stopped at several instants in time and probably exceeded the average speed several times.

Average Speed versus Instantaneous Speed

Since a moving object often changes its speed during its motion, it is common to distinguish between the average speed and the instantaneous speed. The distinction is as follows.

Instantaneous speed: the speed at any given instant in time.

Average speed: the average of all instantaneous speeds. This is found by a distance-to-time ratio calculation.

You might think of the instantaneous speed as the speed that the speedometer reads at any given instant in time and the average speed as the average of all the speedometer readings during the course of a road trip. Since the task of averaging speedometer readings would be quite complicated (and maybe even dangerous), the average speed is more commonly calculated as the distance/time ratio.

Referring back to the illustration of trapezoid, we can infer the following:

Gradient or slope of the triangle segment $= \frac{v - u}{t} = a$

v = final velocity
u = initial velocity
t = displacement time
a = acceleration ($-a$ for the case of deceleration; g = 32 ft/s^2 or 9.80665 m/s^2 for acceleration due to gravity)

If we denote displacement distance by S, we have the following set of equations:

$$v - u = at$$

$$v = +at$$

$$S = \frac{u + vt}{2}$$

$$= \frac{(v + u)}{2} \frac{(v - u)}{a}$$

$$= \frac{v^2 - u^2}{2a}$$

$$v^2 - u^2 = 2at$$

$$v^2 = u^2 + 2at$$

$$S = \frac{u + vt}{2}$$

$$= (u + v)\frac{t}{2}$$

$$= (u + u + at)\frac{t}{2}$$

$$= (2u + at)\frac{t}{2}$$

$$\therefore S = ut + \frac{1}{2}at^2$$

The practical application of the preceding equations and explanations can be seen in a typical soccer training formation as presented in the chapter on training tips.

Maximum and Minimum Points

The maximum and minimum points of a function are useful for determining the placements of the soccer ball in relation to spatial displacement. A function is a mathematical expression that describes a physical phenomenon. For example, suppose the path of the ball is described by the function below:

$$B(t) = -3t^2 + 2t + 3$$

Then, the specific location of the ball at time t (in seconds) can be traced by evaluating the function at that particular time. The maximum point of the function represents the maximum height reached by the ball. The maximum and minimum points are found by taking the first derivative of the function, using the laws of calculus. The process of taking the derivate is called "differentiation," which represents the rate of change of the function. When the first derivative is set equal to zero, the corresponding value of t represents the time when the function reaches its maximum or minimum point. For the example function above, the derivative is:

$$B'(t) = -6t + 2,$$

which, when set equal to zero, yields t = 3 s. Thus, a major use for the derivative of a function is finding the maximum or minimum points of the function. The derivative indicates the rate of change of the function. Specifically, the derivative measures the slope of the function at a particular point as shown in Figure 6.13.

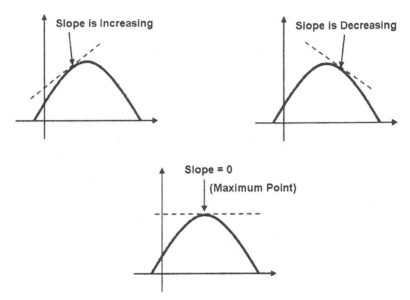

Figure 6.13: Slope and maximum points on a curve

When the slope changes from positive to negative, the function is at its *maximum* when the slope is zero. When the slope changes from negative to positive, it is at its *minimum* when the slope is zero. A low bounce is intercepted (Figure 6.14a) by the opponent, while a high bounce (Figure 6.14b) flies above the opponent. Figure 6.15 shows actual player demonstrations of ball bounce blockage and miss.

Figure 6.14a: Low bounce with ball interception

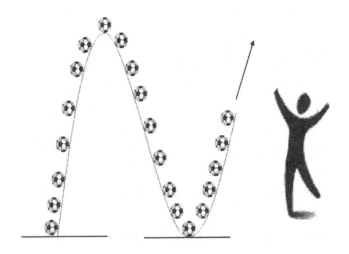

Figure 6.14b: High bounce with no interception

Figure 6.15: Player demonstration of ball bounce blockage
and miss

Basic Calculation Examples

Force

(1) A player kicks a soccer ball that has a mass of 0.45 kg into a goal at a rate of 2.6 m/s in 5s. What is the force on the ball?

$F = ma = mv/t = (.45)(2.6)/(5) = 0.234$ N

(2) A player is practicing kicking a soccer ball at a wall. The ball has a mass of 0.4 kg and is kicked at a rate of 10 m/s in 3 s.

(a) With what force does the ball hit the wall?

(b) What force does the wall exert on the ball?

Answer: $F = ma = mv/t = (0.4)(10)/(3) = 1.333$ N.

Thus, the wall exerts an equal but opposite force (1.333 N) on the ball as shown in Figure 6.16.

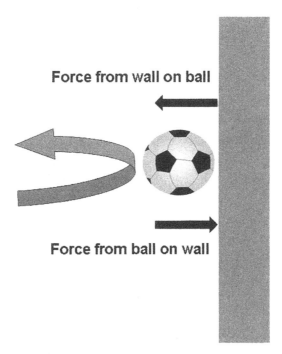

Force from wall on ball

Force from ball on wall

Figure 6.16: Ball bounce on a wall

Friction

A soccer player with a mass of 79 kg slides on the field while trying to kick the ball. During the slide, he was retarded by a frictional force (from the grass on the field) of magnitude 470 N. What is the coefficient of kinetic friction between the player and the ground? Acceleration due to gravity, g, is 9.8 m/s^2.

Procedure

The static friction coefficient (μ) between two solid surfaces is defined as the ratio of the tangential force (F) required to cause a slide, divided by the normal force between the surfaces (N).
$\mu = F/N$
For a horizontal surface the horizontal force (F) to move a solid resting on a flat surface
F= (μ)(mass of object)(g).

If a body rests on an incline plane, the body is prevented from sliding down because of the frictional resistance. If the angle of the plane is increased, there will be an angle at which the body begins to slide down the plane. This is the angle of repose, and the tangent of this angle is the same as the coefficient of friction.

Calculation

$F = \mu_k(N)(g)$
$\mu_k = F/Ng = 470\ N/(79\ kg)(9.8\ m/s^2) = 0.61$

Notice that N (newtons) in the numerator is cancelled out by the newton force (N) in the denominator generated by the player's mass (F = ma).

Gravitation

If a player on offense has a mass of 120 kg and another player 2 m away has a mass of 95 kg,

(a) What is the strength of gravity between them?

(b) What is the strength of gravity between the first player and a ball of mass 0.45 kg when the ball is 40 m away?

Given: Universal constant for gravity, **G**, between two bodies = 6.67 × 10⁻¹¹

$F_g = G \cdot m_1 \cdot m_2/d^2 = (6.67 \times 10^{-11})(120 \text{ kg})(95 \text{ kg})/(2 \text{ m})^2 = 1.9 \times 10^{-7}$ N

$F_g = G \cdot m_1 \cdot m_2/d^2 = (6.67 \times 10^{-11})(120 \text{ kg})(0.45 \text{ kg})/(40 \text{ m})^2 = 2.251 \times 10^{-12}$ N

Projectile Motion

Projectile motion is a common occurrence in soccer. Whether the soccer ball is kicked horizontally, lobbed, or deflected, the principles of projectile motion can be applied. In soccer, both gravity and air resistance direct the soccer ball's trajectory. For simplicity of calculations, air resistance is often omitted in ball trajectory computations. But in reality, the influence of air resistance leads to a smaller projectile range. Thus, the actual trajectory of the ball is not as parabolically symmetric as it is often presented graphically without air resistance. In general, the higher the air pressure, the higher the air resistance. When a soccer ball is kicked, the pressure of the air in front of it increases, leading to an increase in air resistance, which resultantly slows the ball down. Let us consider the computational examples that follow:

(1) A soccer ball is kicked from the ground with an initial speed of 19.5 m/s at an upward angle of 45 degrees, as shown in Figure 6.17. Notice that normal axial resolution (R) of the ball's direction can be calculated from trigonometry as:

$$Y = dSin\theta$$
$$X = dCos\theta$$

(a) Where does the ball land?

(b) How long does it take the ball to land?

(c) Another player who is 55 m away from where the ball was first kicked starts running to meet the ball; what must his average speed be if he is to meet the ball just before it hits the ground?

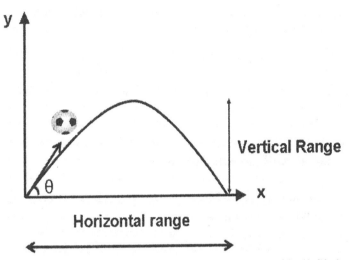

Figure 6.17: Horizontal and vertical ranges of ball flight

Procedure

The horizontal range (R) of projective motion is calculated from the equation[29] below:

$R = 2(v_0^2/g)\sin\theta\cos\theta = (v_0^2/g)\sin2\theta$

Calculation

(a) $R = (v_0^2/g)\sin2\theta = (19.5 \text{ m/s})^2/(9.8 \text{ m/s}^2)\sin(90) = 38.8$ m
(away from where it was initially kicked)

(b) $R = (v_0\cos\theta)$ t; t = $R/(v_0\cos\theta) = 38.8/(19.5\cos45) = 2.81$ s

29. www.pa.uky.edu/~moshe/phy231/lecture_notes/projectile.html

(c) Velocity = change in distance/change in time = 38.8 m – 55 m/2.81 s = –5.8 m/s (The minus sign is because the player is running in the opposite direction to the ball).

(2) During a throw-in, the ball is thrown up by a player at an angle of $\theta = 60$ degrees with respect to the horizontal so that his teammate, who is about 1.8 m tall, could head it. It took the ball 2 s to get to the header.

(a) Find the horizontal distance the ball travels.

(b) What is the velocity with which the ball was thrown?

This problem will be easier to solve if we do a "time-reverse" of the motion. So, we will have the following:

(a) Using $y = v_{0y}t - \frac{1}{2}g\, t^2$; $v_{oy} = (y + \frac{1}{2}\, g\, t^2)\, /\, t = 10.7$ m/s; $v_0 = v_{0y}/\sin60^0 = 12.4$ m/s

(b) $x = v_{0x}\, t = v_0(\cos\theta)\, t = (12.4)\, (\cos60^0)(2) = 12.4$ m

Friction and Air Drag on Soccer Ball

Air friction produces a drag on a soccer ball when it is kicked. The question below illustrates a possible calculation of interest.

Question

What is the terminal speed of a 0.47 kg soccer ball that has a radius of 0.12 m and a drag coefficient of 2.6? The density of the air through which the ball falls is 1.2 kg/m^3.

Solution

Air friction equations[30] are used to solve this problem. Air friction, or air drag, is an example of fluid friction. Unlike usual surface friction, air drag is velocity dependent, which may be very complicated. Only

---

30. www.hyperphysics.phy-astr.gsu.edu/hbase/airfri.html#c3

simplified cases can be treated analytically. At very low speeds for small particles, air resistance is approximately proportional to velocity and always directly opposite the velocity. For higher velocities and larger objects, the frictional drag is approximately proportional to the square of the velocity, as shown below:

$$f_{drag} = -\frac{1}{2} C\rho A v^2,$$

where C is drag coefficient, ρ is air density, A is cross-sectional area, and v is velocity. Since drag is opposite to the velocity, the negative sign in the equation becomes positive for calculating velocity. Thus, we have:

$$v_t = (2 \, mg/C\rho Av^2)^{1/2} = [2(0.47)(9.8)/(2.6)(1.2)(3.142)(0.12)^2]^{1/2} = 8.1 \text{ m/s}$$

Linear Momentum

During a penalty kick, a 0.48 kg ball that was kicked horizontally at 10.4 m/s strikes the goal post and rebounds with a speed 7.2 m/s. What is the change in its linear momentum?

Note: This is a bad kick and the player could not score from it.
The initial velocity is positive and the final velocity is negative because the ball is going in the opposite direction when it rebounds. Therefore, we have:

$$\Delta p = mv_i - mv_f = (0.48)[10.4 - (-7.2)] = 8.45 \text{ kg.m/s}$$

Collision and Impulse

A soccer player kicks a ball of mass 0.45 kg that is initially at rest. The player's foot is in contact with the ball for 0.003 s and the force of the kick is given by:

$$F = [6000000 \, t - 2000000000 \, t^2] \text{ N}.$$

Find the magnitude of (a) the impulse on the ball due to the kick, (b) the average force on the ball from the player's foot during the period of contact, and (c) the ball's velocity immediately after it loses contact with the player's foot.

(a) $J = \int F \, dt = \int [6000000 \, t - 2000000000 \, t^2] \, dt = 9 \text{ N.s}$

(b) $J = F_{avg} \bullet \Delta t; \; F_{avg} = J/\Delta t = (9 \text{ N.s}) (0.003) = 3000 \text{ N}$

(c) Since the ball starts from rest, it acquires momentum equal to the impulse from the kick. So, $v = p/m = J/m = 9/0.45 = 20 \text{ m/s}$

Angular Velocity

The angular velocity is a vector quantity that specifies the angular speed and axis about which an object is rotating. For example, when a spin is put on a soccer ball when it is kicked (e.g., in banana shots), it exhibits an angular velocity as shown in Figure 6.18.

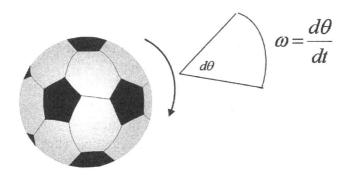

$$\omega = \frac{d\theta}{dt}$$

Figure 6.18: Angular velocity of ball motion

The SI unit of angular velocity is radians per second (rad/s), although it may be measured in other units such as degrees per second, revolutions per second, and degrees per hour. When measured in cycles or rotations per unit time (e.g., revolutions per minute), it is often called the rotational velocity, and its magnitude, the rotational speed. Angular velocity is usually represented by the Greek symbol omega (Ω or ω). The direction of the angular velocity vector is perpendicular to the plane of rotation, in a direction that is usually specified by the right-hand grip rule.

Calculation Involving Rotation

During a free kick, a soccer player can kick a ball with a speed of 11.5 m/s at an angle of 20 degrees to the horizontal and a rotation rate of 65 rad/s. Neglecting air drag, determine the number of revolutions of the ball by the time it reaches maximum height.

At maximum height, the ball's velocity (in the y direction) is zero, so using $t = v\sin\theta/g = (11.5 \text{ m/s})(\sin 20^0)/(9.8 \text{ m/s}^2) = 0.4$ s
Now using $\theta = \omega t = (65 \text{ rad/s})(0.4 \text{ s}) = 26$ rad

Rotation is described in terms of angular displacement, time, angular velocity, and angular acceleration. Angular velocity is the rate of change of angular displacement, and angular acceleration is the rate of change of angular velocity. The averages of velocity and acceleration are defined by the relationships:

$$\text{Average angular velocity: } \bar{\omega} = \frac{\Delta\theta}{\Delta t}$$

where the Greek symbol, delta (Δ) indicates the change in the quantity following it. A bar above any quantity indicates the average value of that quantity.

Work

Work is the result of the application of force. In order to accomplish work on an object, there must be a force exerted on the object, and it must move in the direction of the force. Figure 6.19 illustrates force application in a shoulder-to-shoulder soccer contest.

Figure 6.19: Application of force translates to work

For the special case of a constant force, the work may be calculated by multiplying the distance times the component of force, which acts in the direction of motion.

$$Work = (Force)(Distance)$$

Important principles of work include the following:

Work requires energy.

Power is the rate of accomplishing work.

A force with no motion or a force perpendicular to the motion does not accomplish work.

1 lb-wt is the force by which a body of mass 1 lb is attracted to the Earth.

1 ft-lb force is the work done by a body of mass 1 lb-wt in moving a distance of 1 ft.

Conservation of Linear Momentum

A 95 kg soccer player moving at 4.1 m/s on an apparent breakaway to score is tackled from behind. When he was tackled by an 85 kg player from the opposing team running at 5.5 m/s in the same direction, what was their mutual speed immediately after the tackle?

Assuming there is no external forces, then the momentum p is conserved, so we can use $p = mv$.

Total momentum before collision = momentum after collision. That is,

(95 kg) (4.1 m/s) + (85 kg) (5.5 m/s) = v (95 kg + 85 kg); v = 4.76 m/s

Collisions and Impulse

A soccer ball of mass 0.45 kg was kicked at a speed of 9.3 m/s. The soccer ball was in contact with the player's foot for 0.035 s. Find (a) the impulse imparted to the ball, and (b) the average force exerted on the ball by the player's foot.

Using impulse = $F \Delta t = \Delta p$, we have:

Impulse = (0.45 kg) (9.3 m/s) - (0.45 kg) (0 m/s) = 4.185 kg m/s

Average force F = Impulse/Δt = 119.6 N

A soccer ball of mass 0.48 kg and speed 12.2 m/s strikes the side of a goal post at a 45 degree angle and rebounds with the same speed at 45 degree (shown in Figure 6.20). What is the impulse given to the ball?

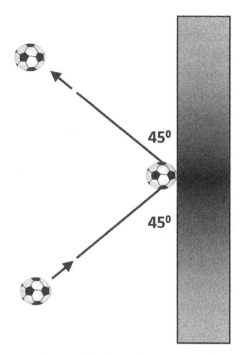

Figure 6.20: Ball ricochet off a goal post

Using impulse = Δp, there is no change in momentum along the y direction, only along the x direction.

$\Delta p = p_{final} - p_{initial} = (0.48 \text{ kg}) (12.2 \text{ m/s}) (\cos 45^0) - (-0.48 \text{ kg}) (12.2 \text{ m/s}) (\cos 45^0) = (2) (0.48 \text{ kg}) (12.2 \text{ m/s}) (\cos 45^0) = 8.28 \text{ kg m/s}$ to the left (negative × direction)

Weight, Height, Inertia, and Balance

Stability is a function of where the center of gravity is located. Because of the lower center of gravity, a shorter object will tend to be more stable than taller ones. Consequently, it would be easier to trip a taller opponent. When weight or mass is thrown into the picture, the cliché of "the bigger they are, the harder they fall" may indeed manifest itself during a game. A heavier body will need more force to overcome inertia. A heavier body in motion will require more force and distance to stop than a lighter body. It takes a great deal of force to stop or change the direction of motion of a fast-moving object. Because momentum is calculated as weight times speed, a heavier player will build up a higher momentum than a lighter player. More force applied on a soccer ball will make it go faster, thus building up more momentum. The higher force applied generates a higher speed, which compensates for the lighter weight of the ball such that a high momentum can still be generated. This principle is why a small bullet traveling at a high speed generates a tremendous force of impact.

Chapter 6 References

Cutnell, John D. and K. W. Johnson, *Physics*, 7th ed., Wiley, Hoboken, NJ, 2006.

Giancoli, Douglas C., *Physics: Principles with Applications*, 6th ed., Pearson Education, Upper Saddle River, NJ, 2004.

Halliday, David, Robert Resnick, and Jearl Walker, *Fundamentals of Physics Extended*, 7th ed., Wiley, Hoboken, NJ, 2007.

Serway, Raymond A., *Physics for Scientists & Engineers*, 3rd ed., Saunders, Philadelphia, PA, 1990.

.

Chapter 7
Physics of the Soccer Foot

Of what use is it to build up all that soccer skill if you don't have a foot to stand on? The foot is a paramount asset for playing soccer. Proper foot care is, thus, very essential for all soccer players. The human foot combines mechanical complexity and structural strength. The ankle serves as foundation, shock absorber, and propulsion engine. The foot can sustain enormous pressure (several tons over the course of a one-mile run) and provides flexibility and resiliency. The foot and ankle contain the following:

- Twenty-six bones (one quarter of the bones in the human body are in the feet)
- Thirty-three joints
- More than a hundred muscles, tendons, and ligaments
- A network of blood vessels, nerves, skin, and soft tissue

Tendons connect muscles to bones, while ligaments connect bones to other bones. All these components work together to provide the body with support, balance, and mobility. A structural flaw or malfunction in any one part can result in the development of problems elsewhere in the body. Interestingly, abnormalities in other parts of the body can lead to problems in the feet.

Foot Note

Structurally, the foot has three main parts: the forefoot, the midfoot, and the hindfoot. The forefoot is composed of five toes (*phalanges*) and their connecting long bones (*metatarsals*). Each toe (*phalanx*) is made up of several small bones. The big toe (*hallux*) has two phalanx bones—distal and proximal. It has one joint, the *interphalangeal joint*. The big toe articulates with the head of the first metatarsal and is called the *first metatarsophalangeal joint* (MTPJ). Underneath the first metatarsal head are two tiny, round bones called *sesamoids*. The other four toes each have three bones and two joints. The phalanges are connected to the metatarsals by five metatarsal phalangeal joints at the ball of the foot. The forefoot bears half the body's weight and balances pressure on the ball of the foot.

The midfoot has five irregularly shaped tarsal bones, forms the foot's arch, and serves as a shock absorber. The bones of the midfoot are connected to the forefoot and the hindfoot by muscles and the *plantar fascia* (arch ligament). The hindfoot is composed of three joints and links the midfoot to the ankle (*talus*). The top of the talus is connected to the two long bones of the lower leg (*tibia* and *fibula*), forming a hinge that allows the foot to move up and down. The heel bone (*calcaneus*) is the largest bone in the foot. It joins the talus to form the subtalar joint. The bottom of the heel bone is cushioned by a layer of fat. A network of muscles, tendons, and ligaments supports the bones and joints in the foot. There are twenty muscles in the foot that give the foot its shape by holding the bones in position and expand and contract to impart movement. The main muscles of the foot are the following:

- Anterior tibial, which enables the foot to move upward
- Posterior tibial, which supports the arch
- Peroneal tibial, which controls movement on the outside of the ankle
- Extensors, which help the ankle raise the toes to initiate the act of stepping forward
- Flexors, which help stabilize the toes against the ground

Physics Inside the Foot

Smaller muscles enable the toes to lift and curl. There are elastic tissues (tendons) in the foot that connect the muscles to the bones and joints. The largest and strongest tendon of the foot is the Achilles tendon, which extends from the calf muscle to the heel. Its strength and joint function facilitate running, jumping, walking up stairs, and raising the body onto the toes. Ligaments hold the tendons in place and stabilize the joints. The longest of these, the plantar fascia, forms the arch on the sole of the foot from the heel to the toes. By stretching and contracting, it allows the arch to curve or flatten, providing balance and giving the foot strength to initiate the act of walking. Medial ligaments on the inside and lateral ligaments on outside of the foot provide stability and enable the foot to move up and down. Skin, blood vessels, and nerves give the foot its shape and durability, provide cell regeneration and essential muscular nourishment, and control its varied movements. With the multitude of parts and components, there is a lot that can go wrong and adversely affect the effectiveness of the foot for soccer-playing purposes. The simple piece of advice is to take good care of the foot so that it can perform at its highest possible level of efficiency. A sketch of the human foot[31] is shown in Figure 7.1, while the internal bone structure is sketched in Figure 7.2.

Figure 7.1: Sketch of the human foot

31.   sportsmedicine.about.com/cs/foot_facts/a/foot1.htm

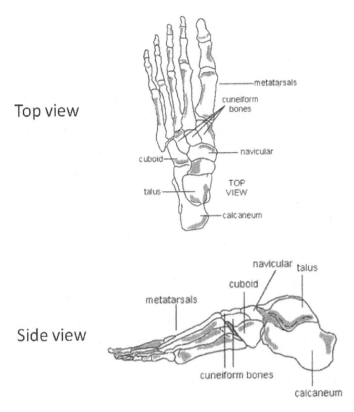

Figure 7.2: Bone structure of the human foot

Foot and Boot

Proper footwear is essential for preserving the integrity of the foot in performing its functions effectively. A "boot," as a soccer shoe is classically known, must be selected for the right size, fit, texture, and comfort. Cutting corners in selecting soccer shoes will only lead to long-term foot problems. Foot and boot work together and must be coordinated to obtain good results. Progressive and degenerative problems can develop from prolonged use of the wrong soccer boots, shoes, or cleats.

Agony of the Feet

Abuse, neglect, and lack of care can quickly lead to agony of the feet, manifested in a variety of foot problems. Most soccer players take the foot for granted. It is only when something goes wrong that they realize that the foot is a natural engineering masterpiece that requires good maintenance. Apart from impact injuries (sprains, strains, and breaks), there are many other problems that can beleaguer the foot. Some of these are summarized below:

Corns and Calluses

Thick and hard areas of skin (calluses) can appear anywhere on the feet where persistent rubbing or uneven pressure occurs. The most common places are the heel, the ball of the foot, and the side of the toes, where flat feet, bunions, or ill-fitting shoes may be responsible. As time goes by, calluses may become cracked and painful or develop into corns. Corns come in two types:

- Soft corns appear between the toes because of unusual pressure.
- Hard corns are found on the top or the end of the toes, or the soles of the feet, and are caused by abnormal pressure.

Plantar Fasciitis

The plantar fascia is a fibrous band that stretches between the heel and the base of the toes. It helps to maintain the structure and shape of the foot. This can often be the cause of severe heel pain. Plantar fasciitis causes small tears to appear on the heel and becomes inflamed and extremely painful. Typically, pain is felt first thing in the morning after getting out of bed but recedes after around thirty minutes as the band is stretched and the swelling is reduced. Pain can also be felt under the arch of the foot after prolonged walking or standing. Plantar fasciitis is more likely if you have the following:

- Flat feet

- High arches
- Weight problems
- Sudden or abrupt involvement in physical activity to which the foot is not accustomed

Plantar fasciitis can get better with rest, but this can take a long time, and the pain can be so severe it prevents some people from walking.

Athlete's Foot

It's not only athletes who get this fungal infection, which grows in warm, moist areas of the body. Between sweaty toes is an ideal home for the fungus, which is usually picked up from swimming pools and communal changing rooms (for example, locker rooms). Athlete's foot makes the skin itchy, red, and sore, and if not treated, the skin soon becomes soggy and starts to crack and peel. The fungus can also spread to the toenails. If the area affected is moist, it should be treated with an anti-fungal spray; if the area is dry, use an anti-fungal cream. In mild cases, powder can be used.

Toenail Problems

During an average month, a toenail grows 0.3 centimeter. White spots can appear following simple knocks to the nail, vertical ridges appear with age, and fungus can invade from the surrounding skin. Avoid pointing anything sharp down the sides of a toenail because it can become infected, leading to a swollen, red, and painful toenail.

Verrucas

These are caused by a virus that infects the skin. They're similar to warts on hands. They can be difficult to spot and are often painless when small. They usually appear as areas of rough skin, sometimes with tiny black spots in them. Most often they're passed around where it's wet and people are walking barefoot, such as at swimming pools and in gym showers. They're easier to treat when small. Salicylic acid treatments can work if they're caught early.

Chapter 8
Brian Peacock's Soccer Training Clinic

This chapter presents a collection of miscellaneous tips for soccer training by Dr. John Brian Peacock (Peacock 2002), a former soccer teammate and professional colleague of the author. Coaches and players are encouraged to pick and choose whichever tips are applicable to their specific team interests.

Counting and Team Groups

- How many players on a team?
    - Any number, but in professional games there are eleven and about five substitutes, which added together, makes sixteen.
    - This is a good number for a squad: it ensures that all players get a fair amount of playing time and leaves the team with enough players when some team members are not available to play.
- How many different kinds of practice games can you play with sixteen players?
    - Any number: 8@1:1, 4@2:2, 2@4:4, 1@8:8.
    - But what about 2:1, 3:1, 3:2, 4:3, and so on?
    - One strategic purpose of the game is for players to move about the field to create these numerical mismatches.
    - Now we have to find something to do with the remainders.
        - If you have sixteen players at practice and play 2:1 games how many players are left out?

Arithmetic: Groups and Combinations

- For the sake of convenience, let us label our sixteen players by the first sixteen numbers or letters of the alphabet:
    - 1, 2, 3, 4, 5, 6, 7, 8, 9, 10, 11, 12, 13, 14, 15, 16
    - A, B, C, D, E, F, G, H, I, J, K, L, M, N, O, P
- Now let us divide the players into groups of four using the colors:

- Red, green, blue, and yellow
- Now the players can keep the same number or letter for the season but they need not keep the same color for every practice. This way, the coach can mix and match the stronger and weaker players.
  - If you really want to complicate the thing, you can assign different roles to each member of a group
    - e.g., Left, right, forward, back
- How many different arrangements of sixteen players can be made?
  - The answer will be given later.

Fun with Poker Chips and Colored Bibs: Randomization

- Get sixteen poker chips—four red, four green, four blue, four yellow—about one inch across (diameter)
- Shuffle the chips on the table and, with a ruler, arrange them in a straight line.
- With an erasable pen, mark them with the first sixteen numbers or sixteen letters of the alphabet.
  - Divide them into groups of four by putting the same color together.
  - Divide them into groups of four with each group having two of one color and two of another
  - Divide them into groups of four with each group having three of one color and one of another.
- If you do this grouping with the player's labels face down, you have true randomization, but if you want to influence the group assignments, then you can arrange them with the player label up.
- You can practice (pseudo)randomization on the practice field by:
  - Lining up the players and drawing out the colored bibs from a bag
  - Having group (color) captains choose their teams
  - Having the coach assign the colors
  - Having players self-select a color/team.

165

- Now you have an easy way of running the practice with groups of four.

Ball Possession Time and Intelligent Play

- If a game lasts sixty minutes, how much ball possession time should a player expect to have?
    - It depends on how many players there are on a team. What if there are eleven players per team, making twenty overall if we leave out the goalkeepers?
    - So each player expects to have 60/20 = 3 minutes. Wow!
    - Now if we assume that the ball is in the air or out of play for thirty minutes, we are down to (60 – 30)/20 = 1.5 minutes per player). Wow again!
    - Now if some players hog the ball and get twice as much of the action than the others, then these ten ball hogs will get two minutes each and the other ten will get one minute each. Wow!
- So why are we tired after a game?
    - Because we do much more work—running—off the ball than with the ball.

This is why a player needs to play intelligently. A player should conserve energy and make the most use of the limited ball possession time. Couple this reasoning with the amount of time a player actually gets to be on the playing field, which would depend on substitution patterns and selectivity of fielding players.

Fours Formation

- If we practice for an hour in groups of four, we will get much more ball time than if we practice in larger groups.
- If we stand in line waiting to run up and kick the ball under the eagle eye of the coach, the chances are we will get hardly any practice at all.

- By practicing in fours, we can play all sorts of combinations: 4 together, 3:1, 2:2.
  - How many different game arrangements can you get using four players?
  - AvB, CvD, AvC, BvD, AvD, BvC—that's six (three, really)
  - A&BvC&D, A&CvB&D, A&DvB&C—that's three
  - A&B&CvD, A&B&DvC, A&C&DvB, B&C&DvA—that's four
  - A&B&C&D—that's one
  - Or A, B, C, D on their own—that's one
  - That makes a total of twelve

Shapes, points, lines, and arrows used in field formations are shown in Figure 8.1 and Figure 8.2. Figure 8.3 shows geometry of field formations using triangles, while Figure 8.4 presents possible, impossible, hard, and easy lines of passing and shooting. Figure 8.5 shows mapping of angles to player formations, while Figure 8.6 illustrates using angles to guide accurate passing. Figure 8.7 shows successive ball movements using angles and shapes, while Figure 8.8 illustrates soccer field measurements over which the player formations are executed.

Don't Just Stand Around

Whichever practice formation is used, players should not stand around in line waiting for something to do. In practice, as in a game, all players should be moving into positions to be the next actor in a developing game situation. That is how you learn the essential "feel" for the game. In the old neighborhood days of street soccer, there was only one ball and varying numbers of players from one to 22. Kids rarely "practiced." They just picked teams and played. If you were on your own, you used the wall to play against or a target to shoot at. When there were more players, it was often useful to assign general areas of responsibility around the field and no one claimed to play on offense or defense. The difference between offense and defense had nothing to do with the particular players. It all depends which side had the ball. If your side had the ball, everybody was on offense and should be expecting the ball to come his way. Similarly, if the other side had the ball, everybody was on defense. That meant moving into a position to prevent one of the opponents from doing his job of trying to be in a position to be the next actor in the game.

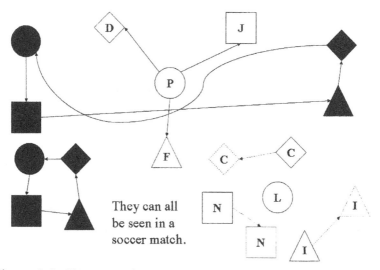

Figure 8.1: Shapes, points, lines, and arrows in field formations

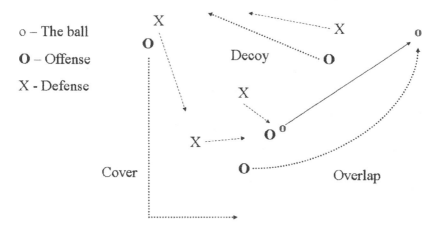

Figure 8.2: Alternate points and lines for field line-up formations

Geometry

- How long is a line?
  - How far can you run, kick, or throw?
- How many players make a triangle?
- How many triangles can you make with four players?

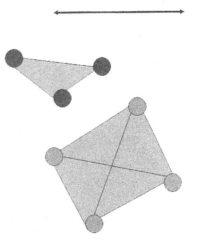

Figure 8.3: Geometry of field formations using triangles

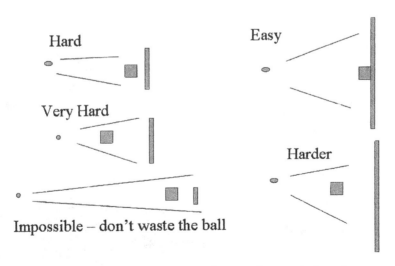

Figure 8.4: Building targets for passing and shooting

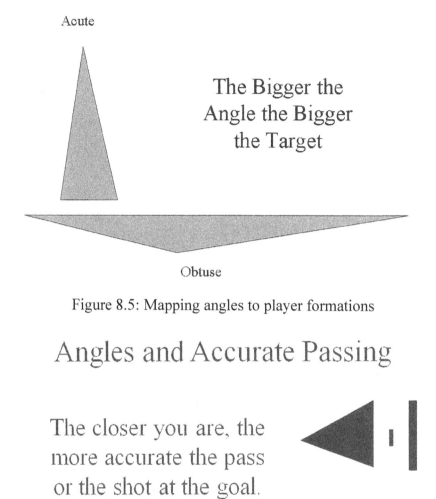

Acute

The Bigger the
Angle the Bigger
the Target

Obtuse

Figure 8.5: Mapping angles to player formations

Angles and Accurate Passing

The closer you are, the
more accurate the pass
or the shot at the goal.

Figure 8.6: Using angles to guide accurate passing

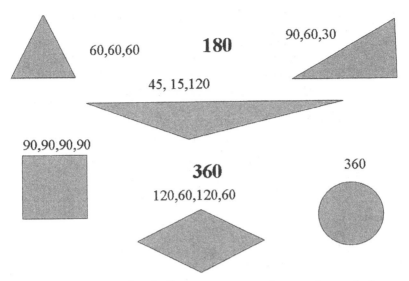

Figure 8.7: Successive ball movements using angles and shapes

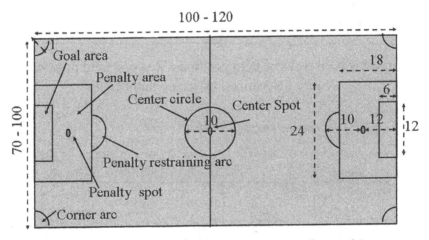

Figure 8.8: Soccer field measurements (in yards)

Soccer Field Area Analysis

Soccer field area analysis, calculations, and player positioning strategies are illustrated in Figures 8.9, 8.10, 8.11, 8.12, 8.13, 8.14, 8.15, 8.16, 8.17, 8.18, 8.19, 8.20, 8.21, and 8.22. Textual information embedded in each figure explains its application.

- The area of a rectangle is the length of adjacent sides multiplied together.
- A square is a rectangle in which all sides are equal.
- The area of a triangle is half the base times the height.
- The area of a circle is the radius times the radius times 22 divided by 7.

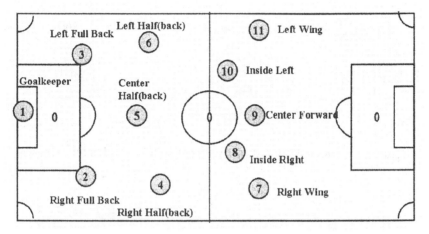

Figure 8.9: Old ways of field positions: Players' field positions were determined by jersey number

On defense, keep between your man and the goal
Wingers, keep wide, Center forward, stay up field
Center half and full backs, stay back and mark your man
Inside forwards and wing, halves run run run.

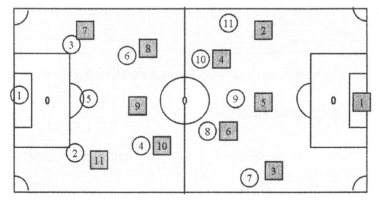

Figure 8.10: Formations for man-to-man marking

The player jersey numbers don't mean anything anymore.
The sweeper plays behind a defensive wall of four.
The wingers and center forward stay up.
Fullbacks overlap on offense and midfielders take the player with the ball.

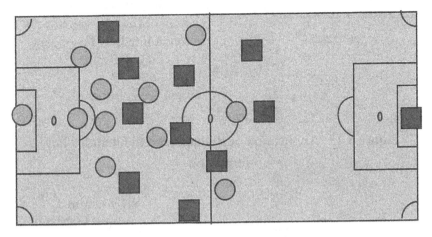

Figure 8.11: Contemporary field formation: Players' jersey
numbers have no relevancy to field positions

They call it Total Soccer.
Two rows of defenders – the front row takes the player with the ball, the
second row act as sweepers.
On offense players rotate, keep possession until
they spot or create a mismatch.

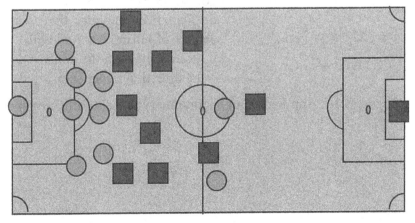

Figure 8.12: Modern formations for Total Soccer era

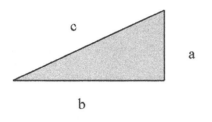

c

a

b

If you are standing on the edge of your penalty area in the middle of the field and your colleague is standing at the junction of the halfway line and the touch line how far do you have to kick the ball?

$$c^2 = a^2+b^2$$

What are a "square" and a "square root"?

Figure 8.13: Application of Pythagorean theorem for field formation

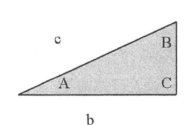

c

B

a

A

C

b

If you aim a corner kick at the penalty spot what is the angle between your kick and the goal line?

If Angle C = 90^0

sine (A) = a/c

cosine (A) = b/c

tangent (A) = a/b

If a is half the width of the goal and b is the shooter's distance from the goal, the chance of hitting the goal with a shot depends on the angle A – the effective target size

Figure 8.14: Application of trigonometry to field formations

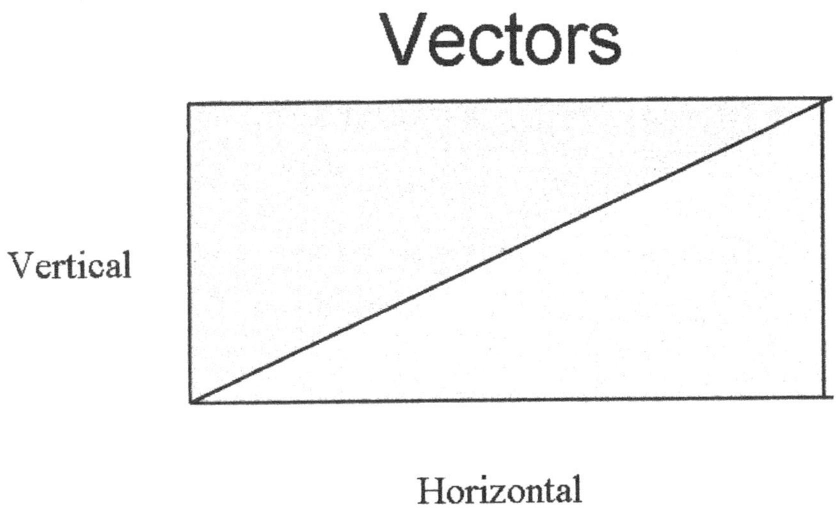

Vectors

Vertical

Horizontal

Figure 8.15: Application of vectors to map vertical and horizontal movements

How far can you kick a ball?

How far can you throw a ball?

How far can you punt a ball?

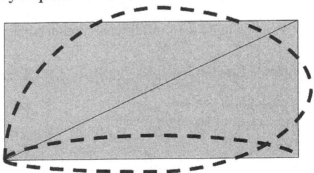

Figure 8.16: Application of trajectories for kicking, throwing, and punting the soccer ball

d = distance		when $u = 0$
t = time	$d = ut + 1/2at^2$	$d = 1/2\ at^2$
a = acceleration	$v^2 = u^2+2ad$	$v^2 = 2ad$
v= final velocity	$v = u+at$	$v = at$
u = initial velocity		

Figure 8.17: Motion equations

d = distance	
t = time	$v=d/t$, $d=v*t$, $t=d/v$
a = acceleration	Miles per hour
V = velocity	Feet per second

$a = v/t = d/t*t$

g = acceleration due to gravity = 32 feet per second per second

Figure 8.18: Additional motion equations

Newton's Laws

An object will remain stationary until acted on by a force.

f= force

m = mass

a = acceleration

$f=m*a$

How much acceleration can you give to the ball ?

How far can you kick the ball ?

Figure 8.19: Application of forces

How high will a ball
bounce?

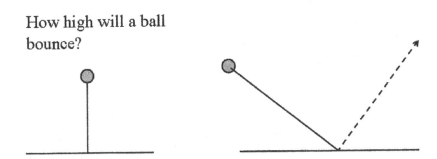

Figure 8.20: Application of elasticity

Pressure

Pounds per square inch (psi)

Pressure and Volume

Boyles Law: The pressure (p) of a
given mass of gas, at constant
temperature, is inversely
proportional to its volume (v)

$$p = \frac{1}{v}$$

How much air should
we put into the ball?

What is the volume of
the ball?

What is the inner
surface area of the
ball?

Figure 8.21: Application of pressure

Differences and Ratios

If two teams finish the season with the same number of points, the
winner may be chosen by goal average or goal difference.
Team A scores fifty goals and gives away twenty-five goals:
Goal average = 50/25 = 2
Goal difference = 50 – 25 = 25
Team B scores twenty goals and gives away five goals:
Goal average = 20/5 = 4

Goal difference = 20 − 5 = 15

If we use average, the defensive team B wins; if we use difference, the offensive team A wins. What should we do?

Probabilities

If we shoot a hundred times from outside the penalty area, we may score ten times. The probability of scoring is 10/100 = 0.1. A "probability" is a number between 0 and 1 and is the ratio of the number of successes to the number of attempts.

If we shoot a hundred times from inside the penalty area, we may score fifty times. The probability of scoring is 50/100 = 0.5.

Probability of a Win

Why doesn't the best team always win? Generally speaking, the best team has the most shots at goal, but the probability of a shot going in is very small and variable, depending on a variety of factors, including skill, accuracy, angle, distance, etc. Say team A has 1,000 shots on goal over the whole season and scores 50 goals in 25 games. That is an average of 40 shots per game, one goal for each 20 shots, and two goals per game. Team B has 750 shots and scores 75 goals in 25 games. That is an average of 30 shots per game, one goal for every 10 shots, and three goals per game. Given this information, what is the probability that Team A will beat Team B assuming the teams take 40 and 30 shots, respectively? This is left as an interesting exercise for motivated readers to solve. Hint: Use the properties of Binomial Distribution from Statistics.

Heart Rate

Our resting heart rate is between 50 and 80 beats per minute. When we run hard during a game, it will increase to between 120 and 200 beats per minute. If we play a lot of sports, our resting and exercise heart rates will go down because our hearts will get stronger and beat harder, thus pushing out more blood per beat. Some professional players have been clocked at an average of over 150 beats per minute over a whole game, with some brief resting periods where it drops to about 20 percent above resting value.

The Heart Itself

The heart takes in blood through the right auricle, pushes it through the mitral valve to the right ventricle, then sends it to the lungs to take up oxygen and give off carbon dioxide before returning to the left auricle, through the tricuspid valve into the left ventricle, and from there it circulates through the muscles, organs, brain, and skin.

The Lungs

There is about 21 percent oxygen in the air we breathe in and about 16 percent in the air we breathe out. If we run hard and breathe in and out twenty times a minute and use four liters of oxygen per minute, how much total air do we need to breathe in on average in a single breath?

Muscles

- The strength of our muscles is related to the cross-sectional area.
- If the diameter of our thigh is eight inches and that of our upper arm is four inches and we can do a fifty-pound curl, how much could we lift by straightening our knee?

Moments

- The farther a weight is from the point of attachment of a muscle, the harder it is to lift.
- The quadriceps muscle attaches about two inches below the knee joint, and the biceps (and brachialis) muscle attaches about one inch below the elbow, but the quadriceps has a cross-sectional area that is four times that of the upper arm.

- If our forearm is twelve inches long and our lower leg is fifteen inches long, what will be the ratio of the moments that we can exert with our arm and our leg?

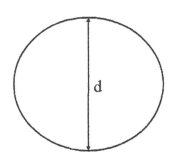

d = the diameter

r = the radius = half the diameter

c = the circumference = d*22/7

a = the area = r*r*22/7

π(pi) = 22/7

If the center circle has a diameter of 20 yards what is its area?

If your thigh is 6 inches across, what is its cross sectional area?

Figure 8.22: Calculation of the area of a circle for field formation

Chapter 8 Reference

Peacock, J. Brian, "Soccer and Science," March 2002.

Chapter 9
Brian Peacock's Seventeen Steps of Soccer Training

In the soccer world of Dr. J. Brian Peacock, there are seventeen key things to learn about the game. These steps show that the strategic use of squares has important application in the motions of offense, defense and practice. The steps are excerpts from Peacock's soccer training manual titled "Seventeen Steps to Supersonic Soccer using Squashed Squares: The Numbers and Pictures" (Peacock 2002).

Squares and Triangles

For many years, coaches have talked about triangles when it comes to offense. Triangles give the player with the ball three options: pass to one or the other of his teammates or take the ball forward himself. But what if he loses the ball? There should always be someone trailing the person with the ball. Similarly, from the defensive point of view, there should always be someone behind the player who is confronting the player with the ball. In this way, we have what systems engineers call "redundancy." Other people would call it belt and braces or belt and suspenders. The other two defensive players do double duty. They cut off passing avenues and position themselves to receive the ball should their colleague obtain possession. So in every play, there should be (at least) four players on each team who have a possibility to contribute to the next step in the game.

If you ever watch a soccer game, whether it be a hoard of seven-year-olds or national professional teams in the World Cup, you will be able to see what happens when you look for the squares (or the absence of squares). You may not see perfect squares; sometimes they get a bit squashed and even look more like a "Y," but you should be able to find four players (for each side) in a position to participate in the next step of the game.

You will remember learning about squares in your geometry lessons. Well, these squares don't always have equal-length sides or right angles at the corners, but they do teach the player important lessons. One lesson is about the length of the sides. It is no good having sides of the squares that are too long or too short, otherwise it either won't be possible to reach the other player with a pass or everybody will get too close and be in each other's way. The important lesson is that the players should learn to judge how far away they should be from the person with the ball (or the person defending the person with the ball).

While we are in the business of geometry, we can ask the question: How many triangles in a square? There are four. Now what if we make two (or three) squares with six people? Then we have twelve triangles. With two lines of four people, we have seven squares and twenty-eight triangles, and that's when it starts to get complicated, and that's why it's such a great game. A great way to learn about soccer strategy and cover is to play a slow motion game with coins on a table top.

Now let us move from geometry to arithmetic. If a game lasts ninety minutes and there are twenty-two players, then on average each player has the ball for $90/22 = 3$ or 4 minutes, or less, if you subtract the time that the ball is out of play or on its way from one player to the next. So why are players so tired after a game in which they only have the ball for a few minutes? Because the most important player in the game is the one who is going to get the ball next (either on offense or defense), and because you don't always know who that will be, you had better get into a good position to be that person. If you look at the heart rates of good soccer players, you will see that they are two or three times their resting rate for most of the game, with occasional relaxation periods when the ball is out of play. Although your share of the ball may be only two or three minutes, your job is to always be involved.

If there is one thing I hate, it is to see players standing in a line at practice, waiting to do something. In practice, as in a game, all players should be moving into a position to be the next participant in a developing situation. That is how you learn the essential "feel" for the game. When I was a little boy, we only had one ball (often a tennis ball) and various numbers of players, from one to twenty-two. We rarely "practiced," we just picked teams and played. If you were on your own, you used the wall to play against or a target to shoot at. When there were more players, it was often useful to assign general areas of responsibility around the field, but woe betide anyone who said he played on offense or defense. The difference between offense and defense is nothing to do with the particular players—it all depends on which side has the ball. If your side has the ball, everybody is on offense and should be expecting the ball to come their way. Similarly, if the other side has the ball, then everybody is on defense; that is, moving into a position to prevent one of the other team from doing his job: trying to be in a position to be the next participant in the game.

We'll talk more about the strategic use of squares later, but first we have another use for squares: practice.

Squares in Practice

Squares are a very useful and instructive way of running a practice session. Almost every kind of practice session can involve groups of two, four, eight, or sixteen players. I believe that sixteen players is enough for any team; any more reduces playing time to unreasonable levels. When I used to play, substitutes were unheard of. You played the whole game, and if someone got hurt, you played with ten.

The ideal equipment for a practice session is one ball and one cone for each two players, and four sets of four differently colored bibs. It would be much better if every player has a ball, a cone, and a bib. Now, let's go back to arithmetic. How many ways can you make use of four sets of four different colored bibs? Well, you can have greens, blues, yellows, and reds playing together; you can have two reds play two greens or three yellows and a blue. The coach with an imagination can mix up the players in many different ways for different exercises and mini games. We can even use soccer to teach arithmetic and geometry.

Pairs

The first exercise should involve pairs of players just kicking the ball to each other, with their right and left feet, at varying distances apart: from about five to twenty meters and then back to five meters. Just keep the ball moving until each player has kicked the ball at least fifty times. You don't really have to teach children of any age how to kick a ball; if they do it often enough, they will learn. It may be useful to put a cone in between each pair so that the players can aim at it, around it, or over it. You don't have to pick up the cone every time it gets knocked over; it won't run away and will still be a good target.

The next variation on this pairs game is to have the players move around their cone in circles of different sizes and in different directions. This way, passers will learn to pass the ball in front of a moving colleague, which is most important when the game gets going for real. A variation is to have the pairs move up and down the field passing the ball to each other. This way they will learn for themselves that the game is much easier if they use both feet. Now with all this kicking going on, we didn't mention stopping the ball. Well, it just happened without us thinking about it. Again, it doesn't matter how you stop the ball, if you do it often enough, you will learn to do it well. You will also learn to link stopping the ball with the next move: kicking it.

A fun pairs game is to start facing each other about twenty meters apart and kick the ball alternately, with the object of getting the ball over the opponent's goal line. This teaches the players how to kick the ball hard and far and makes them run. We'll see more about the big "S"—stamina—later. By the way, you can allow the players to punt or throw the ball instead of kicking it, or you can have one punt and the other throw or kick, and so on. Don't worry about foul throws—two feet on the ground, hands evenly on each side of the ball, which must be delivered from behind and over the head—they will learn. Anyway, they might be fledgling goalkeepers. Whoops! We spent the last paragraph learning more about stopping a bouncing ball without even thinking about it!

Still, in pairs the players can learn about dribbling and tackling. If there is only one cone between two players, they can alternate defending and attacking the cone. Two cones, placed ten or twenty yards apart, can become two goals—first to ten wins. There's even more to this pairs stuff. When the coach blows the whistle, players change partners and carry on with their kicking, passing, stopping, running, dribbling, tackling and shooting games. Before you know where you are, the practice session will be over, every player will be tired, they will have kicked the ball a few hundred times, they will be a little better at the game, they will have had a lot of fun, they have only had to think about one other player, and nobody had to stand in line.

Here's a fun game. Line the players up facing each other in pairs about twenty yards apart, one ball between each pair, a cone next to each player. The game is to knock down your opponent's cone. Every few minutes, stop the game, move each player one position to the left (or right), and then continue. The end player will have to cross to the other side. Don't worry about knocked down cones; they will not run away. Keep the play moving. Try the game with the cones farther apart—that will make them run.

Squares Again

For this activity, you need four players, one ball, and two or four cones. It might be useful to select two players with one color bib and the other two with another, but it doesn't really matter. You start by making a small square about five yards across and have the players keep the ball moving in any direction around and across the square, first-time kicking or stopping with one foot and kicking with the other. You can alternate which foot does what, but the key is to keep the ball moving. Put the cones in the middle and have the players kick around or over them. Enlarge the size of the square, but keep the ball moving. Have the players pass the ball and then move to another corner of the square. Keep the ball moving. Enlarge the square again. Keep the ball moving. You get the idea. Ten minutes of this, and the players will have stopped and kicked the ball a whole bunch of times and have worked their heart just like it should be working in a game.

Take turns putting one of the four in the middle to act as a docile defender. The other three keep the ball away from the player in the middle and keep the ball moving. The player in the middle doesn't tackle or even try to intercept but does give the others something to think about. Later, the player in the middle becomes more aggressive and tries to intercept. But don't forget to keep the ball moving and use both feet. By the way, change the player in the middle from time to time.

Make two goals about twenty yards apart—a single cone will do. Play two on two. After a few minutes, rotate the pairs so that they play against other opponents. Keep the ball moving. Run off the ball into a clear position for your partner to pass to you. Try dribbling around your opponent every now and again. Stop the play; tell every player to race around the goal post at the end of the field and then back to their mini pitch. There's nothing like sprinting and racing to get the blood moving and create some fun.

Opposing Squares

Play four-on-four mini games. Think about getting into position to receive the ball and don't forget the trailing player—behind the player with the ball and the player who is confronting the player with the ball. Every few minutes, blow the whistle and ask each player to say what he is doing and where he is going next. This is called "heads-up soccer." It makes the players think about the squares and about what is happening in the game. If you do this too often, the players will complain that you are interrupting their fun. A great lesson for coaches is to allow the players to play and keep out of the way most of the time. Remember that with eight players in a mini game, each player only gets the ball about one-eighth of the time but they should be running all of the time. This four-on-four level is probably the optimal level of competition. Don't forget to swap the teams around so that the mini teams play against different opponents and with different colleagues. But keep reminding them of the importance of moving off the ball and covering the player with the ball. Once the players have mastered this kind of competition, they are ready to go.

Kicking Experiment

How high can you kick the ball? Assume that you are going to kick the ball straight up in the air. For the time being assume that there is no air resistance. Your partner has a stop watch which he starts when you kick the ball and stops when the ball hits the ground.

Let:

h = the height
t = the time the ball takes to reach its highest point
u = the initial velocity of the ball just after it has left your foot
v = travel velocity of the ball
Let u = 30 ft/sec
When the ball reaches its highest point, v = 0
g = the acceleration or deceleration due to gravity
g = 32.2 ft/sec^2 or 9.81 m/s^2
Note that gravity is "negative" as the ball goes up and "positive" as it comes down.

Using the equations of motion, we have the following three equations:

1. $h = ut + 1/2\ gt^2$
2. $v^2 = u^2 + 2gh$
3. $v = u + gt$

Using equation 3, we have 0 = 30 −32.2 t. Thus, t = 30/32.2 seconds
Using equation 2, we have 0 = 900 − 2[32.2(h)]. Thus, h = 13.98 feet
Using equation 1, we have h = 0 + (1/2)(32.2t^2). Thus, h = 13.98 feet

Thus, the ball will take the same amount of time to come down as it did to go up and when it hits the ground it will be traveling at the same speed as it started.

Human Energy Production and Fatigue

- Physical work is force times distance
    - Ft-lb or joules (1 J = 1 Nm)
- Energy: an object has energy if it has the capacity to do work
    - Joules (1 J = 1 Nm)
    - Kinetic energy (energy due to motion) = ½ mv²
    - Potential energy (energy due to location) = m × g × h joules or weight × h ft-lb
    - Mechanical equivalent of heat: Joules constant J = 4.2

- Power: the rate at which energy is used or work is done
  - Watt: 1 watt = 1 J / s
- Physiological work
  - Mechanical work + heat
  - Kilocalories (1 kcal = 1,000 calories)
  - Kcal/min

Physiological Work and Energy Expenditure

- On a bicycle, the mechanical work done can be measured quite accurately, as there is very little postural (non-value-added) work done.
- Running is less efficient in that the body "wastes" energy by vertical movement.
- Manual materials handling requires that we move both the body and the object.
- More energy is spent during acceleration and deceleration than during steady-state motion.
- Kicking the soccer ball expends energy.

More on units

- 1 kcal/min
- = 70 watts
- = 0.2 liters of oxygen/min
- = 3.6 ml/kg/min
- = 0.8 mets

1 met is the equivalent to the resting metabolic rate of an average male or female.

Energy measurement in Joules

- Coordinated muscle contraction
- Stored as food
- 1 calorie = the amount of heat needed to raise the temperature of 1 gram of water 1 degree C

- 1 kilocalorie (physiological calorie) = the amount of heat needed to raise the temperature of 1 kg of water 1 degree C

Generation of Energy

- Eat
- Breathe
- Turn food into glucose
- Circulate the glucose and oxygen to the muscles
- Send signals from the brain to the muscles, which contract
- Produce meaningful coordinated physical work, like playing soccer or surfing the Internet

Citric Acid Cycle

In aerobic organisms, the citric acid cycle, also known as the Krebs cycle, is part of a metabolic pathway involved in the chemical conversion of carbohydrates, fats, and proteins into carbon dioxide and water to generate a form of usable energy. In addition, it provides precursors for many compounds including some amino acids and is, therefore, functional even in cells performing fermentation. While it is not necessary for a soccer player to understand the intimate details of the citric acid cycle, it suffices to know that eating the right types of food at the right time helps to generate desired levels of energy.

Measurement of Physical Work

The following items have impacts on physical work:
- Food
- Oxygen
- Circulation
- Muscle contraction
- Activity
- Fatigue
- Body temperature
- Perceived strain
- Excretion

- Level of performance
- Training effect
- Mechanical work

Work capacity declines with working time, as illustrated in Figure 9.1. A very fit person can work at 50 percent of maximum aerobic capacity for eight hours per day, six days per week. A general recommendation is 33 percent for an eight-hour shift, 30 percent for a ten-hour shift, and 25 percent for a twelve-hour shift. Some experts are more conservative in order to "protect" a greater proportion of the working population.

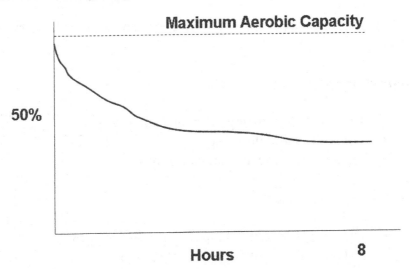

Figure 9.1: Aerobic capacity over hours of work

How Hard can a Person Play?

A commonly accepted maximum energy demand level for continuous work (i.e., work carried out over a full day with normal rest breaks) is around 5 kcal/min. This is equivalent to the energy cost of an average person walking at about 3.5 MPH. A British postal worker guideline (Jones 1970) indicated an expected level of 6 kcal/min. Brian Peacock's parcel-handling study confirmed this rate with male subjects aged twenty-three to fifty-one (Peacock 1980). At the other end of the spectrum, Nag (1987) suggested that a level of 15 kcal/min was a "reasonable load and rate of work" for workers in India who were accustomed to heavy work.

Limiting Factors

- Fitness
- Motivation
- Rewards
- Fatigue
- Age and sex
- Health

How much should a person eat? What goes in must go out; otherwise it is stored.

Impact of Eating

- 1 gram of carbohydrate contains about 5 kcal
- Protein is about the same
- 1 gram of fat contains about 9 kcal

Impact of Respiration

- Outside air contains about 20.9 percent oxygen
- Expired air contains about 16 percent oxygen
- We measure the volume of expired air, measure the oxygen content of a sample, and estimate the amount of oxygen used over a period of time
- Oxygen debt

Impact of Temperature

Ambient temperature as well as body temperature can affect the performance of a player. Soccer players, at most levels of exertion, need extra hydration for proper health and performance. Sweating is necessary in order to maintain constant body temperature. The sweat rate usually corresponds to increases in energy expenditure by the athlete. Trained athletes have a more sensitive sweating system than nonathletes due to adaptation over time. Body temperature is affected by the following:

- Percentage used toward mechanical energy generation
- Percentage that is dissipated as heat
- Processes of conduction, convection, evaporation
- Environmental conditions
- Clothing
- Workload

Factors Affecting Individual Maximum Energy

- Expenditure Capacity
- Body size: 5 kcal/min for every 20 kg weight
- Age: 1 percent per year after the age of twenty-five
- Sex: females = 80 percent males
- Level of conditioning: up to 20 percent improvement
- Motivation: it varies a lot!

Big Bang and Big Crunch

Most of the universe consists of space. Even atoms, which have a nucleus of protons and neutrons, with a bunch of shells of circulating electrons, are mostly just space. In the beginning, all these atoms were crushed together, with hardly any space between them, then there was a Big Bang, and all the atoms and combinations of atoms making up molecules and stars and planets started to spread out. At the beginning of a soccer game, all the players congregate around the coach, touch hands, and either chant a slogan or make a prayer for success. Then the Big Bang happens: all the players spread out around the field to their own positions, run around in circles for ninety minutes, and then, if they win, converge in a big pile to celebrate their victory—we can call this the big crunch. There is very little space between the players, and they are united in ultimate success, until next week!

This big bang/big crunch theory of the universe may differ a little from a soccer game. First, when the players play the game, they are constrained by the touchlines and goal lines, only occasionally venturing outside. The time is limited to ninety minutes. They are also constrained in other circumstances, like staying outside the center circle at kickoff, staying outside the restraining arc while a penalty is being taken, staying ten yards from the ball during a free kick, and providing enough space for the goalkeeper to kick the ball or for a throw-in to be taken. Does the universe have limits or will it expand forever? Will the big crunch happen? When? Is the ball like gravity—attracting all the players together? Just watch a bunch of eight-year-olds! What forces move the players into their own space?

The laws of soccer are intended for it to be a noncontact sport—each player has his own personal space. Every now and again, these laws are broken—the goalkeeper may have to fight for his space during a corner kick, defenders fill space, and attackers try to create space. Every now and again, an allowable collision occurs, shoulder to shoulder, with just enough force to create a little space. Where the shoulder charge is too violent or where other kind of contact occurs—pushing, tripping, kicking, holding—then the referee blows his whistle and the game starts with everyone in their own bit of space.

Now in the universe, collisions between planets, stars, asteroids, and other bits of space junk result in a big commotion, just as it does on the soccer pitch. There is a lot of energy wasted and heat generated. In fact, big collisions—like the one that may have happened a few million years ago—killed all the dinosaurs. You may also have seen the movie *Armageddon*, where the hero defied gravity (there is not much gravity on little asteroids) and blew an asteroid apart and sent it off to bypass the earth. It would have been a real shame if our hero had failed; we might have had to cancel Saturday's soccer game.

The Seventeen Steps

It is now time to move on to the seventeen steps to supersonic soccer using squashed squares, according to Brian Peacock's doctrine. The use of squares in the game and in practice will occur at each step.

The seventeen steps are listed below. Note that the seventeenth step recommends knowing the seventeen official laws of soccer. The "17-on-17th" format is not a circular reference. It is rather an example of Brian Peacock's effective practice of mnemonic referencing. The steps are:

1. Build stamina

2. Build strength

3. Get speed

4. Acquire and use skill

5. Look and see

6. Shout – The sound and fury of soccer

7. Use space

8. Take shots

9. Set plays

10. Keep it short and simple

11. Play safe

12. Save the ball through goalkeeping

13. Develop game strategy

14. Share the ball

15. Simulate game scenarios

16. Be a good sport

17. Know the seventeen official laws of soccer

Stamina

Why do people play soccer? Some who are good enough play to make a living, but most play to have fun, and many play to keep fit. There is probably no other game that stresses the cardiovascular and respiratory systems as much as soccer. It is even more strenuous than running. Why? The answer comes from mechanics. The energy cost of accelerating, decelerating, starting, and stopping is much greater than that consumed by running at a steady pace. And soccer is all about sprinting; stopping; turning; moving forward, sideways, and backward; and jumping and falling down (sometimes) and getting up and pushing (so long as you do it shoulder to shoulder), and so on. When you've played a full game of soccer, you have probably raised your heart and respiration rates to close to their maximum for much of the game. The good players are still running hard at the end of the game. A good practice should keep everybody moving most of the time. Do not have players standing in line waiting to do something.

During practice, you can start slowly, passing the ball backward and forward between pairs or among squares. But soon, you must accelerate the practice by having players move after they have passed the ball into a new position to receive the ball back. A simple game is to have twos or fours move in circles of varying sizes, keeping the ball moving. Don't forget to pass the ball in front of the receiving player. Next, you can run around the pitch in your groups keeping the ball moving all the time. Blow the whistle. Leave the balls where they are and everyone runs hard around two goal posts (or to two touchlines and back to their ball). That will get the heart going.

If you want to work on stamina without the ball, you can do repeat sprints: line up at one end of the pitch, jog to halfway, sprint to the other goal line, turn, wait for everybody to catch up, jog back to halfway, sprint to the goal line. Repeat five or ten times. If you get similarly talented runners to stay near each other, you can add the incentive of racing to work on those lungs. By the way, coach: you should join in! It would be good for you, and you'll get the respect you deserve.

There are literally hundreds of variations on this theme. Have the players do shuttle runs. Have races within and among the groups.

Drop to the ground and stand up halfway through each run. Use the cones. Have the player leap over a cone and head an imaginary ball. If you want, use the ball during the runs. Kick the ball, throw the ball, carry the ball, but above all, keep everybody moving. Stamina wins games. Standing in line listening to the coach doesn't do anything for stamina and probably doesn't do much for other aspects of the game.

Now, let's see about that homework. There is no reason why anyone shouldn't run a few miles a day. Why do parents drive their children to practice at the local school that is only a mile or two away? Run or walk with them, it will get easier once you have made it a habit. Now if it is raining, you may think that you will be able to skip that stamina homework. Did I say "skip"? Let's get back to physics and gravity. If you accelerate your body up against gravity, you use a lot of energy, especially if you keep it going for twenty minutes or more. Also, skipping is fun. If you don't have a rope, then just jump up and down a couple of hundred times. Probably the best stamina training is to play four-on-four for a couple of hours a few times a week. In addition, just keep running.

Strength

Strength and stamina go hand in hand. Exercises like running, jumping, skipping, and stopping and starting make legs strong. You need strong legs to kick the ball hard and far. But there is also a physics technique for building leverage for hard and long kicks. A big wind-up of a long leg does not necessarily generate high kinetic energy on the ball. A short and stocky player using proper techniques can generate more kicking power on the ball than a tall player. This is because short and fast kicks that connect with the ball at the right point can contribute more to kinetic energy than massive long-legged kicks.

Probably the best way to develop the strength to kick the ball a long way is by kicking the ball a long way a lot of times. It is great fun to have kicking competitions in pairs or fours—kick the ball alternately and try to move your opponent back to his own goal line. Players should alternate between left and right feet. For a change, punt or throw the ball, and use one hand or two. Don't always run forward. Try backward and skipping sideways. Walk on all fours—either facing up or down. Play "crab soccer." Jump as high as you can—at least ten or more times. There are other ways of developing strength, but they all require work. Squats, sit-ups, and push-ups are all familiar and have a place in any strength-training routine. If you can reach the crossbar or there is a jungle gym close by, add in pull-ups. Be careful that the goal doesn't fall over.

Strength training involves resisted muscular activity, and what better resistance is there other than your playing buddy, providing you are about the same size. Do arm wrestling. Have pushing and pulling competitions. Lift and carry your partner. Do squats with your partner on your back. Have push-up and sit-up competitions. Try squat thrusts and burpees: Bend your knees, touch the floor, and then jump up as high as you can at least ten times. Then progress to the following: bend your knees, and with your hands on the floor, jump your legs backward then forward and then jump up and repeat, repeat, repeat.

Just look at how strong the pros are. The very good ones can kick or throw the ball more than half the length of the field. In this case, strength of arms and legs dominates the game.

Speed

The difference between top players and those less gifted or practiced is the speed at which they do things. They get to the ball quicker, they control the ball quicker, they kick the ball faster, and they seem to be able to think faster. One practical example of the advantage of speed is that the first player to the ball usually wins the tackle. Another is that the first player into an open space provides a good target for a passer. Finally, the fastest runner will move around and away from an opponent and into open space more quickly. Speed is important, but sometimes the cliché "more haste, less speed" applies. You should always have your brain in gear before you set your feet in motion! This takes practice.

There are two basic measures of human performance: accuracy and speed. Accuracy means that you achieve your objective, and speed means that you do it quickly. Sometimes, there are speed-accuracy tradeoffs. Most children of all ages like to run races, because it is usually clear who the winner is, and because most people eventually come across someone faster than themselves, losing isn't a big deal—it just makes you try harder next time or choose the right opponents.

In practice, coaches should make use of races to improve speed. The races may be of any distance—from five yards to the length of the pitch. They can involve turns around the cones or shuttle runs. They can be forward, sideways, or backward. They can use two feet or hands and feet. They can involve jumps, swerves, falling down, and getting up. They can even involve the ball. You can kick the ball with one foot or both, alternating feet. You can kick it a long way ahead or keep close control. For a change, you can carry the ball or throw it up in the air and catch it. Races can involve two or more players in shuttle runs, ball control runs, and reciprocal passing races at various distances apart. Races rule. They are fun. And races develop speed in all aspects of the game. Even the coach can join in. Most practices should include races of one kind or another. They are intrinsically motivating.

Skill

This is what it is all about. All players possess skills, but some have more than others. Some have different skills. Skill in soccer is about connecting your brain to your feet, via a bunch of nervous-system connections. There is a simple truism about skill. The more you practice, the more skillful you will become at the thing you are practicing. In fact, it is possible to continue to improve speed and accuracy over millions of practice cycles. But there is a complication. It is possible to learn bad habits and repeat mistakes. It is also possible to focus on just a few skills to the exclusion of others. Good players have a wide variety of skills and can play in any position. There is one famous exception that proves this rule. One of the greatest players of all time, Stanley Mathews, couldn't (or didn't) kick the ball with his left foot, rarely headed the ball, and hardly ever scored a goal. But he was a brilliant right winger who regularly tied the left fullback in knots and, to use a term that postdates his playing era, was responsible for many "assists."

How can you measure skill? There are two ways: accuracy and speed. Accuracy means that you do what you planned to do—like scoring a goal, making a successful pass, getting the ball under control, or tackling an opponent. Speed is a measurement of the time it takes to do these things. The complicating thing about skill is that the transaction usually has to be completed in the context of opponents, ground, and weather conditions. It's one thing to be able to juggle the ball with your feet, head, and knees a hundred times; it is an altogether different challenge to receive a high ball with your back to the goal and a defender close behind you, chest it down, turn, and shoot past the advancing goalkeeper. There are two theories about the acquisition of skill. The first is that you learn the elements individually, then put them together, and finally do them under game conditions. The alternative theory is that you practice game situations and the skills are acquired incidentally. I happen to think that the latter approach is more fun and, therefore, likely to be more successful in the long run.

There really are only four kinds of skill in soccer: ball control, tackling, kicking, and strategic use of these elements. Ball control skills involve the process of receiving the ball from any direction and at any height and at any speed, dribbling it, and preparing to pass or shoot the ball. Tackling is all about timing. There are a few guidelines that are worth mentioning up front. Watch the ball, not your opponent's feet or eyes. Either get in quickly before your opponent has control of the ball or hang back a little and wait for your opponent to give it to you. Surprisingly, the latter strategy is often more successful. The kicking skill is basic and can only be acquired through practice, practice, practice. You can kick the ball with any part of your foot: inside, top, outside, toe, or heel—they all have their place. Kicking skills are best learned through mini games of shooting and passing, not by listening to the coach tell you how to kick.

The square is a good way of practicing ball control skills. The four players should just pass the ball about as the square gets bigger and smaller and changes shape, rotates, and progresses around the field. The key rule to this practice of ball control and kicking skills is to tell the players that the ball must not stop. You can play first-time passing or two- or three-touch. As the control skills develop, players will control the ball and move it into a position for the next pass all in one movement. A fun game is to have one of the four players act as a passive defender in the middle while the others move about and keep the ball in motion. It's surprising how often a passive defender will get the ball on an interception. A progression of this game is to allow the defender to become more aggressive, but then you will often find that it is easier for the three to keep the ball away.

Now, we move on to kicking. As I said earlier, the ball may be kicked with any part of the foot, but players will usually get more distance and accuracy if they use the "instep": the top inner side of their foot. Generally, the nonkicking foot is placed next to the ball, and the head and shoulders are over the ball. But kicking a soccer ball is like hitting a golf ball; there are many variations on the theme. If you want the ball to go hard and low, you put your body over the ball. If you want to lift it in the air, you should approach the ball at an angle of up to 45 degrees, place your stance foot a little farther away, lean back a little, and undercut the ball. You can make the ball swerve by hitting it with the outside or inside of the foot. Players should practice all of these variations as they pass the ball around the square. Perhaps the best kicking practice is a one-on-one or two-on-two in which the teams kick the ball alternately with the aim of getting the ball to the other goal line. One thing to remember: If the ball is passed along the ground, it makes the receiver's control task much easier than if the ball is bouncing.

Look and See

Great players have eyes "in the back of their heads," so to speak. In technical terms, they have good situational awareness. Players should practice looking around and listening to their teammates calling for the ball. One way of encouraging situational awareness skills is for the coach to blow the whistle to stop playing during practice games. Each player then has to say what he is going to do next and what the other players are going to do—both teammates and opponents. Players should be encouraged to play with their heads up. The next part of seeing is anticipating: predicting where your teammates and opponents are going to move in the next few seconds.

Shout—The Sound and Fury of Soccer

A natural partner to seeing is shouting or using other signals to attract the attention of a teammate. A potential receiver should shout the name of the ball player as he moves into position. Alternatively, a third player should shout the name of an open receiver. Pointing or raising your hand or making eye contact with a colleague are all ways of helping. There is a fine line between legal tactical shouting and "verbal obstruction." You should always shout a name and not things like "my ball" or "square ball." You should not shout if you are not in an open position. Shouting that is aimed at deceiving the opposition may be penalized.

Use Space

The effective use of space is the most important tactical part of the game. Space is somewhere where you or a teammate is and your opponent isn't. When you get more advanced in your analysis, space is where you, your teammate, or the ball is going to be in the next few seconds. In the early days of traditional formation—two fullbacks, three halfbacks, and five forwards—the players had fairly rigid territories. But as the game has progressed, the job of a player is not to cover his designated opponent or area of the field. Rather, it is to move strategically with the play, move into open space, and always remember the need to cover the player who has the ball.

Whatever basic lineup is adopted, players will find themselves participating in various squares that cover the field. A typical situational square will include the player with the ball, two teammates within fairly close passing distance, and a fourth player behind him. A change in the direction of the play will find players participating in a different square. The defensive counterpart of the offensive square is that there should always be a player between an offensive player and the goal.

Three-on-one or two-on-two games are great ways of making players find space. Again, it is often good to play with passive defense; the team without the ball doesn't tackle—they just look for interceptions. The passer should pass the ball in front of a moving colleague. Good players like an opponent to commit to a tackle—it gives them a better opportunity to dribble around him or pass the ball. One thing on slide tackling, a very important part of the game at the right moment: you must get the ball and not the player. You must also remember that you will end up on the ground and, therefore, will be out of the play if your tackle is not successful.

As players become more experienced, space can be created by decoys and strategic shielding through placing your body between your opponent and the ball. But pushing off will get you called for obstruction.

Take Shots

Shooting at the goal is the occasional end result of a long build-up around the field, and because it is so occasional, it is important not to squander the opportunity. The trick is to increase the probability of a successful outcome: scoring a goal. The first rule of shooting is to get close enough to the goal; the closer you are, the better your chance of scoring. It is rare for children to score from outside the penalty area because they can't kick the ball hard enough. Even the professionals only have a 50/50 chance of scoring from outside the box if the goalkeeper is in a satisfactory position to see the ball coming. There are two reasons for not shooting from too far away: space and time. The space thing is that the target (the goal) is relatively smaller the farther you are away, so that a shot from close up will go just inside the post, one with the same angular direction from farther away will miss the goal. The second problem is time; the more time you give the goalkeeper to see the ball coming and move into its path, the more likely it is that he will save it. Therefore, the first rule of shooting is to get in range!

The second rule is to choose as big a target as possible so as to reduce the chance of missing the goal and the chance of the goalkeeper stopping the ball. The target is the space around the goalkeeper—above and to the side—but within the goal posts. Note that it is generally harder for a goalkeeper to reach a low ball than a high one. It takes him a longer time to dive and move his hands to the bottom two feet of the goal than to the upper six feet, assuming that the goalkeeper is six feet tall. But if small children play in full-size goals, then it makes sense to kick the ball over the goalkeeper's head. If the goalkeeper advances to "narrow the angle," then you should shoot toward the side with the biggest gap (often the far post). When you become excellent at the game, you may be able to lob the ball over the head of the advancing goalkeeper, which takes a lot of practice, as you have to learn to control the trajectory by hitting the ball just hard enough; otherwise, the ball will go over the crossbar.

As players become more skillful at kicking, they will become more adept at "bending" the ball around the advancing goalkeeper. If you want to swerve the ball to the right, hit it with the outside of your right foot or the inside of your left foot, and vice versa. Also, if you want the ball to dip, then you hit the ball with the inside of the foot with a glancing upward blow, so as to impart topspin.

The ball is rarely stationary when the player is about to shoot, except for a penalty kick or a free kick. The shooter has more time to prepare for his shot if the ball is rolling toward him than if it is delivered from the side or behind. Thus, the golden rule for the assisting player is to play the ball back to the shooter or, if there is sufficient space between the shooter and the goalkeeper, to place the ball in front of the shooter so that he can run onto it. This kind of pass is a low-probability one, as the advancing goalkeeper will have more chance to come out of his goal and narrow the angle. It is difficult for a player to receive a ball from behind, but it is even more difficult to receive a bouncing ball, because the shooter will have to time his movement to the ball more precisely and may have to control the ball first and then shoot.

Shooting, like any skill, can only be improved by practice, practice, and more practice. There is no value for a dozen or so players standing in line waiting for their turn to shoot. Perhaps the best form of shooting practice is in groups of four players. Place two cones to make a goal, have one player act as goalkeeper, two in front and one behind, and practice passing and shooting nonstop.

Rotate the players frequently. With this practice form, it is possible to demonstrate the effectiveness of different forms of assist: coming back toward the shooter, coming from behind, and bouncing. Another level of practice is to have one of the pair in front of the goal provide passive defense so that the shooter has to move sideways to get a clear shot at the goal. If he scores, then the goalkeeper can turn and provide passive defense for the new shooter who was standing on the other side of the goal.

Set Plays

There are quite a few stoppages in soccer, such as when the ball goes out of bounds, when a foul has been committed, or when the game restarts after a goal. Quite a few strategies have been tried after a kickoff. One interesting one is to boot the ball as far forward as possible. Of course, this gives the ball to the opposition, but at least the play will continue to the other team's goal. The more common, conservative tactic is to retain possession by passing the ball to a colleague standing close who, in turn, passes the ball back to a halfback; then the midfield possession game can start. There are other more risky and innovative starts such as passing the ball directly to a winger, dribbling the ball upfield, or passing back followed by a kick upfield to attackers who have had time to run into a position where they have at least a 50/50 chance of receiving the ball. Note that the ball must travel forward from the kickoff. This rule is an anachronism and really serves no useful purpose.

Before the change in rules regarding goal or dead ball kicks, it was common for the goalkeeper to pass the ball sideways to a fullback who then returned it to the goalkeeper. The goalkeeper would then advance to the edge of the penalty box, bouncing the ball every four steps, before booting it upfield. Nowadays, this tactic is not allowed and is not really an issue except for young children because the balls used have a greater coefficient of restitution and can be kicked much farther than the old, soggy leather balls. Also nowadays, goalkeepers can usually reach at least the halfway line with a goal kick and often well into the opponent's half with a punt. A few other things have changed and mostly for the better. Those heavy, soggy balls would not bounce well on a soft, muddy goalmouth, and this gave rise to all sorts of odd situations and encouraged attackers to confront the goalkeeper. Indeed, shoulder charges on the goalkeeper used to be allowed and even encouraged. Clever attackers would stand in front and slightly to one side of the goalkeeper so that he couldn't punt the ball with his preferred foot (usually the right one). A big no-no was raising your foot in front.

Keep It Short and Simple

Keep it short and simple (soccer KISS) is good advice for passing the ball, provided teammates are effectively positioned. A high-probability pass into good space is better than a 50/50 ball to a colleague who is closely marked or a long hopeful boot upfield. But when the ball is in your own penalty area, don't play about, get it out of there. In the old days, a pass back to the goalkeeper was an important and perfectly legitimate way of playing it safe. But some teams abused this strategy in order to waste time. So the law was changed to disallow the goalkeeper from using his hands from a direct pass (with the foot) by a colleague. This doesn't mean that you shouldn't pass back, only that you run a greater risk of losing the ball if you do. But remember to always pass back wide of the goal, in case the goalkeeper misses the ball.

Wherever possible, pass the ball to a colleague along the ground, because a bouncing ball is harder to bring under control. Shoot from in front of the goal and not from a narrow angle. If you are out toward the wing and approaching the goal, pass the ball back toward a colleague running into the penalty area. He will have a better chance of scoring than you. Passing the ball is usually better than trying to dribble it around an opponent, unless that opponent is not covered, in which case you have more space to play with. Don't try to develop complex sequences; remember that fours are about as much as our minds can deal with quickly and effectively.

Play Safe

Playing safe, particularly on defense, is of great importance. Clear the ball out of your own penalty area. Don't pass across your own goal in your half of the field, as this will often lead to an interception and no defensive cover. Pass to a close colleague who is not marked. Play the game in your opponent's half of the field. Always have someone covering the player with the ball, usually about five to ten yards, so that if he is tackled, there is a good chance that the covering player will be able to regain possession quickly. Forwards are responsible for defense. They must come back and cover behind the player who is challenging for the ball. There is usually no hurry to get upfield, unless you have drawn the opponent's defense out of position. Unless you are a genius, try to get the ball under control before you do something else. Again, remember to pass to a nearby colleague who is not marked. Pass into clear space, but don't provide 50/50 passes and get your teammate creamed.

Goalkeeping

Goalkeeping is a special skill that relies on anticipation and agility. Narrow the angle. The key to effective goalkeeping is to provide the smallest possible target to the opposing players by advancing off your goal line. Be careful not to come out too quickly or too far, as this will provide your opponent with the chance to lob the ball over your head. Always cover your near post when the attack is coming from a wing. Keep your legs together or go down on one knee to provide a solid wall. When going out to meet an opponent who is in the clear, dive sideways to block as much of the goal as possible. Catch the ball rather than punch it. From corner kicks, start on the far post and move out and forward toward the ball. You don't want to let it go over your head. Remember that if the ball is in the goal area, you should consider it yours.

Distribute the ball to a player who is in the clear. It is often better to throw the ball to an unmarked player out toward the wing rather than boot the ball upfield. Also look for a winger who is coming back for the ball close to the halfway line—he will often be unmarked.

Another ploy is for a midfielder to run into space toward the touchline, thus providing a large, unmarked target area. As the last resort or when you have the wind behind you, boot the ball downfield as far as you can. Such a kick is especially effective on hard ground when the ball bounces high.

Game Strategy Development

There are three levels of control of a game:

- **Ball control:** Executing the basic skills like kicking, dribbling, and tackling.

- **Tactical play:** Creating space and passing into space and using the wind, sun, and ground conditions to your advantage. The player who has a knack for doing this on the fly during a game is sometimes called the "schemer."

- **Strategic play:** Carrying out preplanned attacking moves and defensive cover. Play on your own team's strengths and the opposing team's weaknesses.

Play long balls into the wind and square balls when the wind is behind you in your opponent's half, as this will prevent you from giving the advancing goalkeeper an easy job. Curl the ball into the goal with the wind from the wing and use the wind to make the ball move away from the goalkeeper. Present the goalkeeper with high bouncing balls on hard ground. Play long balls over the head of the opposing fullback into space for your winger to run into. Pull the ball back for a colleague who is following up. Never give the goalkeeper an easy ball to intercept or catch.

Overlap by rotating the cover player out toward the wing while making sure that someone else fills in behind the player with the ball. Forwards, run out toward the wing to spread the defense, thus creating large holes. Get into a position for a pass. Come back and wide for a throw from your goalkeeper. Send a player upfield as a decoy while another comes across for the ball.

Share the Ball

The biggest crime in soccer is to hold onto the ball when a colleague is in a better position to shoot or progress up the field. Soccer is a game of sharing. There are superstars but the best players are team players. Running off the ball, covering a player who has moved upfield, providing a good target for a pass, and not shouting when you are in a marked position are all ways that the player without the ball can share and help the player with the ball to share. There are other ways of sharing, such as warning a colleague of an opponent behind him, always getting back to help the defense when you have lost the ball, and congratulating a colleague who makes a good play (shot, tackle, run into space, or a pass). Most of all, be quick to forgive and forget mistakes made by a colleague. After all, nobody intends to make a mistake, and your turn may be next.

Simulate Game Scenarios

It is easy to simulate the game with poker chips on a table. Work on set plays and defensive and offensive strategies. Always look for the squares, with one player trailing the player with the ball. Show how decoys and overlaps create space.

Being a Good Sport

Soccer is a great game; some people call it a sport. The players, coaches, officials, and spectators should be "good sports." If you play long enough, you will win a few games and lose a few, especially if you progress or gravitate to your own skill level. Of course, the purpose is always to win, but if you won every time, you would soon lose interest in the game because there would be no challenge and therefore no sport. If you foul an opponent deliberately, stop the ball with your hands, or protest a referee's decision, you are missing the whole point of the game. Coaches, referees, and teammates should be particularly vigilant regarding the following bad behaviors: jersey pulling, loose elbows, deliberate tripping, pushing in the back, tackling through the ball, charging or kicking the goalkeeper, shouting to distract an opponent, or acting offensively in other ways. Do not retaliate; this will usually get you in bigger trouble than the initial offense. Do not argue with officials, coaches, opponents, or spectators, since they all usually do their best to play the game. Remember that referees may often play the advantage rule and thus ignore even a deliberate foul. Do not criticize your teammates' mistakes. Coaches, don't tell the player that he messed up. He didn't intend to and probably feels bad enough already without your help. Soccer is a game of skill and serendipity. Sometimes, the play goes as intended, but more often it doesn't.

Know the Laws of the Game

Below are the seventeen standard and official regulations of soccer that represent the whole scheme of the game. The regulations are called the "Laws of the Game." They are established by FIFA, and changes are approved annually at the meeting of the International Football Association Board (IFAB). The seventeen official laws are:

1. The field of play

2. The ball

3. The number of players

4. Player's equipment

5. Referees

6. Linesmen

7. Duration of the game

8. The start of play

9. Ball in and out of play

10. Method of scoring

11. Offside

12. Fouls and misconduct

13. Free kick (direct and indirect)

14. Penalty kick

15. Throw-in

16. Goal kick

17. Corner kick

Most of these laws don't really matter, and neither do the thousands of pages of "decisions of the international board (FIFA)." If you really want to learn about them, you can obtain a copy on the Internet, buy one of many books on soccer, or through your local association. And I suppose if you want to avoid arguments, then you should read the laws and the interpretations.

Why Game Laws?

Laws are general guidelines that are intended to provide order in the game and provide safety for the players. The "decisions" or rules are more rigid interpretations that are needed to resolve disagreements regarding the laws. Millions of children all over the world play happily by interpreting the laws (which they have never read) with common sense.

The "field" is any fairly flat surface with one or two goals. The size of the field and goals depends on how many players there are, how big the players are, and how big the ball is. A regular tennis ball on a patch of concrete provides a venue for endless soccer fun. Even law #12, "Fouls and Misconduct," is really common sense. Don't use your hands and kick the ball, not your opponent.

Even in the top level of soccer, the job of the officials is to keep the game moving and only interfere when a player may gain an unfair advantage by contravening one of the laws. But people play the game, and people are competitive and like structure, especially when it is important which team wins. So we are stuck with all these interpretations.

Despite all the decisions of the international board and a variety of local rules by well-meaning administrators, there is still room for on-the-spot interpretation. Was the trip incidental? Was the handball accidental? Was the player in an offside position actually interfering with play? Was the ball completely over the line? Did the goalkeeper move before the penalty kick was taken? (Usually!) Is the defensive "wall" ten yards away from the ball until a free kick is taken? Is a slide tackle or a jumping tackle dangerous? (Sometimes.) Was a shoulder charge too robust? Was a throw-in performed "correctly"? Did the offending player gain an advantage from his misconduct? Was the action malicious? Who was to blame—the high kicker or the low header? Is high kicking a crime? Was the shielding fair or obstructive? Efficient referees make these judgment calls all the time, and capable players accept their decisions, even if they are wrong.

Chapter 9 Reference

Peacock, J. Brian, "Seventeen Steps to Supersonic Soccer using Squashed Squares: The Numbers and Pictures," 2002.

Chapter 10
Soccer Calculations

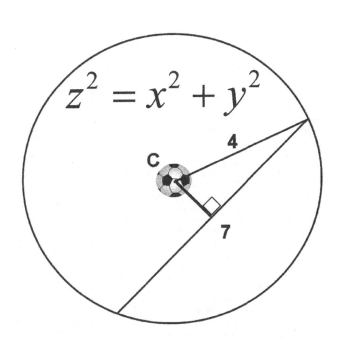

$$z^2 = x^2 + y^2$$

C

4

7

Physics calculation examples in this chapter are adapted from the author's own previous collections (SFC 1972) and several published sources, including Mitiguy and Woo (2005) and Lowe and Rounce (2002). The problem context has been modified in each case to fit soccer game scenarios.

Bisection of Angles

In the images in Figure 10.1 and Figure 10.2 below (not drawn to scale), $x = 60$ and $y = 40$. If the dashed lines bisect the angles with measures of $x°$ and $y°$, what is the value of z?

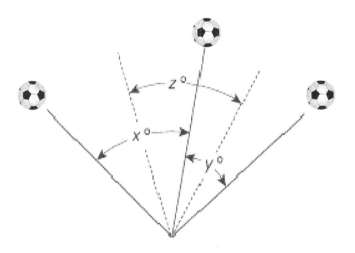

Figure 10.1: Bisection of Angles Image 1

A. 25
B. 35
C. 40
D. 45
E. 50

Answer: E

First, add the labeled points A, B, C, D, E, and O to the figure, as shown below. Then segment $\overline{OB}$ bisects $\angle AOC$, so $m\angle AOB = m\angle BOC$, and $m\angle AOB + m\angle BOC = x° = 60°$. Thus, $m\angle AOB = m\angle BOC = 30°$. Similarly, $m\angle COD = m\angle DOE = 20°$, because $\angle COD$ and $\angle DOE$ are of equal measure and the sum of their measures is $y° = 40°$. From the figure, it follows that $z° = m\angle BOC + m\angle COD = 30° + 20° = 50°$. Therefore, $z = 50$.

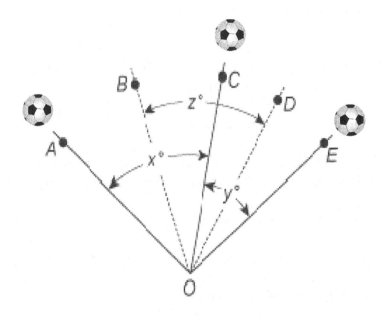

Figure 10.2: Bisection of Angles Image 2

Line Segment Comparison

Although a line segment is check-marked sequentially at points A, B, C, D, and E and we are given the following relationships: $AB < BC < CD < DE$, which of the following must be true based on the line segment relationships?

A. $AC < CD$
B. $AC < CE$
C. $AD < CE$
D. $AD < DE$
E. $BD < DE$

Answer: B

You can rewrite AC as $AB + BC$, AD as $AB + BC + CD$, CE as $CD + DE$, and BD as $BC + CD$, and then consider the five answers. The first choice is equivalent to $AB + BC$ is less than CD. You know that AB is less than CD and that BC is also less than CD, but the sum of AB and BC might not be less than CD. Since the question asks which statement *must* be true, the first choice is not the correct answer. The second choice is equivalent to $AB + BC$ is less than $CD + DE$. This statement must be true, because AB is less than CD and BC is less than DE. Although there is no need to consider the other answers once you see that the second choice must be true, each of the remaining choices could be rewritten in the same way, and you could see that they need not be true.

Rectangle Length Comparison

The length of rectangle S is 20 percent longer than the length of rectangle R, and the width of rectangle S is 20 percent shorter than the width of rectangle R. Based on this information, the area of rectangle S can be inferred to be:

A. 20 percent greater than the area of rectangle R
B. 4 percent greater than the area of rectangle R
C. Equal to the area of rectangle R
D. 4 percent less than the area of rectangle R
E. 20 percent less than the area of rectangle R

Answer: D

Let's represent the length and width of rectangle R as x and y. Then the area of R is xy. The length of rectangle S is 20 percent longer than x, which is $x + 0.20x$, or $1.2x$. Similarly, the width of S is $y - 0.20y$, or $0.8y$. The area of S is $(1.2x)(0.8y)$, which simplifies to $0.96xy$. From this it follows that the area of rectangle S is 4 percent less than the area of rectangle R.

Rectangle within Practice Circle

In Figure 10.3 (not drawn to scale), Point A marks the center of the practice circle from where soccer practice passes originate while Points B, C, D, and E mark the positional options for teammates receiving the passes. Point B is twelve feet from A and Points A, B, C, and D are located at the corners of a rectangle. Point E is eighteen feet from B. How long is line segment BD?

A: 18 feet
B: 20 feet
C: 30 feet
D: 12 feet
E: 42 feet

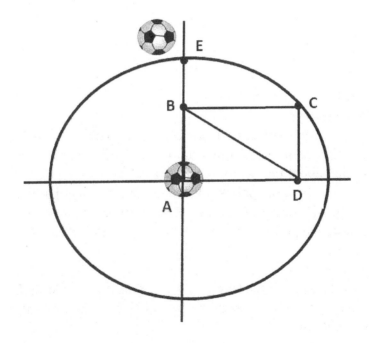

Figure 10.3: Rectangle within Practice Circle

Answer: C

217

Note that the shape ABCD forms a rectangle. Thus, BD and AC must be the same length, representing the diagonal of the rectangle. But AC also represents the radius of the practice circle. Thus, AE and BD are equal. Based on the given data that AB is twelve feet and BE is eighteen feet, the radius of the circle is twelve feet + eighteen feet = thirty feet. Consequently, BD = thirty feet.

Line Segment Units

A, B, C, and *D* are points on a line, with *D* the midpoint of segment BC. The lengths of segments AB, AC, and BC are 10, 2, and 12, respectively. What is the length of segment AD?

A. 2
B. 4
C. 6
D. 10
E. 12

Answer: B
Solution Steps
The key to this question lies in *not* jumping to incorrect conclusions. The question names the points on a line. It gives us a variety of information about the points. The one thing it *does not* do is tell us the order in which the points fall. Some may assume that the order of the points is *A*, then *B*, then *C*, then *D*. But as we will see, if we try to locate the points in this order, we would not be able to answer the question.
Points of Interest
The question asks for the length of line segment AD. In order to find this length, we have to establish the relative positions of the four points on the line.

Given Data
Drawing the figure would help as shown in Figures 10.4a, 10.4b, 10.4c, and 10.4d. We might be tempted to locate point *A* first. Unfortunately, we don't yet have enough information about *A* to place it correctly.

We can place *B, C,* and *D* because *D* is the midpoint in Figure 10.4a.

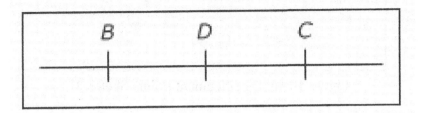

Figure 10.4a: Line Segment Points Sketch 1

We know the lengths of three of the line segments:
AB = 10
AC = 2
BC = 12
Because we know where BC is located, we can label the length of BC (Figure 10.4b).

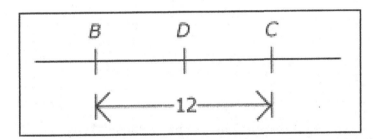

Figure 10.4b: Line Segment Points Sketch 2

Now, construct the figure by adding what we know and what we can figure out. Because *D* is the midpoint of BC, we know that BD and DC are each 6 units long (Figure 10.4c).

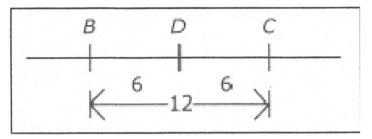

Figure 10.4c: Line Segment Points Sketch 3

Where can we place point *A*? It has to be 2 units from *C*, because AC = 2. It also has to be 10 units from *B*, because AB = 10. So, the only location for *A* is between *B* and *C*, but closer to *C*. Place point *A* and mark the distances. We can now figure out the answer to the question. DC is 6 units. *A* is 2 units closer to *D* than *C*, so AD is 4 units (Figure 10.4d).

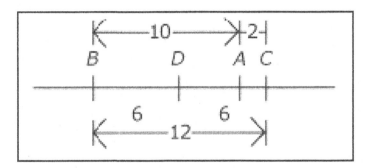

Figure 10.4d: Line Segment Points Sketch 4

Size of Line Segment

In triangle **ABC**, the length of side BC is 2 and the length of side AC is 12. Which of the following could be the length of side AB?

A. 6
B. 8
C. 10
D. 12
E. 14

Answer: D

By the triangle inequality, the sum of the lengths of any two sides of a triangle must be greater than the length of the remaining side. So, BC + AB > AC or 2 + AB > 12. Thus, AB > 10, which eliminates options (A), (B), and (C). Also, by the triangle inequality, BC + AC > AB, or 14 > AB, which eliminates option (E). Therefore, only option D, 12, could be the length of a side.

Triangle Overlap with Circle

The circle shown in Figure 10.5 (not drawn to scale) has center O and a radius of length 5. If the area of the shaded region is 20, what is the value of x?

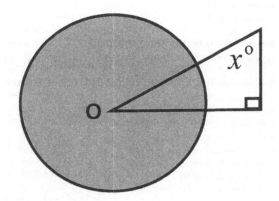

Figure 10.5: Triangle overlap with circle

A. 18
B. 36
C. 45
D. 54
E. 72

Answer: A
Solution
In order to find the value of x, we should first determine the measure of the angle that is located at point O in the right triangle. To determine this angle, we must calculate what fraction of the circle's area is

unshaded. The radius r of the circle is 5 and its area is πr^2, or 25π. The area of the shaded region is 20π, so the area of the unshaded region must be 5π. Therefore, the fraction of the circle's area that is unshaded is given by the expression below:

$5\pi/25\pi = 1/5$. A circle contains a total of 360 degrees of arc, which means that 1/5 of 360 degrees, or 72 degrees, is the measure of the angle at point O in the unshaded region. Since we now know that two of the three angles in the triangle measure 72 degrees and 90 degrees, and that the sum of the measures of the three angles is always 180 degrees, the third angle must measure 18 degrees. Therefore, $x = 18$.

Ball in a Circle

The circle in Figure 10.6 has its center at C. Given segments of the following lengths 6, 7.0, 7.5, 8.10, and 12, which is the length of the longest line segment that can be placed entirely inside the circle?

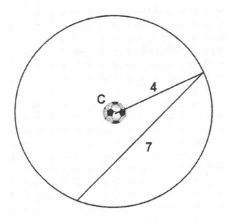

Figure 10.6: Ball in a circle

Solution Logic

Since the radius of the circle is 4, the diameter of the circle is 8. In a circle, the diameter is longer than any segment that can be placed entirely inside the circle. Therefore, segments of length 8.10 or length

14.00 could not be placed entirely within the circle, and the correct answer is 7.5.

Soccer Practice Squares

In Figure 10.7, the large rectangle is divided into six identical small squares. If the perimeter of the large rectangle is 30, what is the perimeter of one of the small squares?

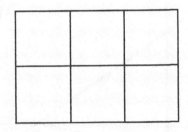

Figure 10.7: Soccer practice squares

Solution

The perimeter of one of the small squares can be found if we know the magnitude of its sides. Let each side of the small square be represented by x. Then the perimeter of the large rectangle is calculated as:

$3x + 3x + 2x + 2x = 10x$, which we know is equal to 30.

Therefore, solving for x yields x = 3. Consequently, the perimeter of one of the small squares is $4 \times 3 = 12$.

Sharp Turn Angles

The angle of a turn during a soccer game can have a serious and direct implication on how the game plays out. Sharp turns versus obtuse turns can be practiced so well that the soccer ball is kept in strategic motion paths. In Figure 10.8, if *PQRS* is a quadrilateral and *TUV* is a triangle, what is the sum of the degree measures of the marked angles? This can be used to map out how a player moves from one point to the other on the soccer field.

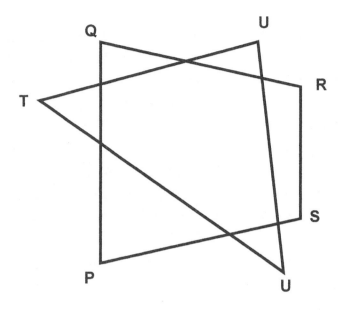

Figure 10.8: Sharp turn angles

In the figure above, if *PQRS* is a quadrilateral and *TUV* is a triangle, what is the sum of the degree measures of the marked angles?

A. 420
B. 490
C. 540
D. 560
E. 580

Answer: C

The marked angles in the figure are angles *P*, *Q*, *R*, and *S*, which are the angles of a quadrilateral, and angles *T*, *U*, and *V*, which are the angles of a triangle. The sum of the degree measures of the angles of a quadrilateral is 360, and the sum of the degree measures of the angles of a triangle is 180. Therefore, the sum of the degree measures of the marked angles is 360 plus 180, which is 540.

Tangent Circle Formations

In Figure 10.9, the circle with center A and the circle with center C are tangent at point D. If the circles each have radius 10, and if line l is tangent to the circle with center A at point B, what is the value of x?

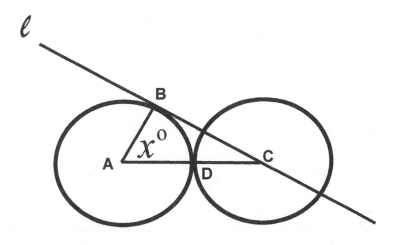

Figure 10.9: Tangent circle formations

A. 55
B. 60
C. 63
D. 65
E. It cannot be determined from the information given.

Answer: B

The circles each have radius 10, so $AB = AD = DC = 10$. Since the circles are tangent at point D, segment contains D and $AC = 20$.

Also, and are perpendicular because a line tangent to a circle forms a right angle with the radius at the point of tangency. Therefore, *ABC* is a right triangle with hypotenuse 20 and side of length 10. A right triangle with one side of length one-half that of its hypotenuse is a 30° – 60° – 90° triangle. The 30° angle is opposite side, so *x* = 90 – 30 = 60.

Height and Shadow

Soccer player, DJ, shown in Figure 10.10, is 180 centimeters tall. At 2 PM one day, his shadow is 60 centimeters long, and the shadow of a nearby soccer corner flag post is *t* centimeters long. In terms of *t*, what is the height, in centimeters, of the flag post?

A. $t + 120$
B. $2t$
C. $3t$
D. $60\text{-}t$
E. $60\text{+}t$

Answer: C

The problem is pictured below, where *x* is the height, in centimeters, of the flag post. There are two right triangles in the figure. One triangle is formed by part of the line from the sun to point *P*, the perpendicular from DJ's head to the ground, and DJ's shadow along the ground. The other triangle is formed by part of the line from the sun to point *P*, the perpendicular from the top of the flag post to the ground, and the flag post's shadow along the ground. Since these two right triangles share the acute angle at *P*, they are similar triangles. Since the corresponding sides of similar triangles are in proportion, it follows that $180/x = 60/t$. Solving this equation for *x*, the height, in centimeters, of the flag post, yields $x = 3t$.

Figure 10.10: Height and shadow

Inscribed Triangle

In Figure 10.11, inscribed triangle *ABC* is equilateral. If the radius of the circle is r, then the length of arc *AXB* is what?

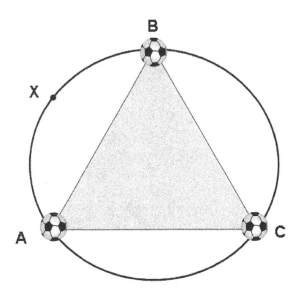

Figure 10.11: Inscribed triangle

A. $2\pi r/3$
B. $4\pi r/3$
C. $3\pi r/2$
D. $\pi r^2/3$
E. $2\pi r^2/3$

Answer: A

An equilateral triangle has three equal sides, so the lengths of the three arcs must be equal, and thus, each arc is 1/3 of the circumference of the circle. The circumference of the circle is $2\pi r$, so the length of arc AXB is 1/3 of $2\pi r$, or $2\pi r/3$.

Chapter 10 References

Jones, Trefor T., "Consumers and productivity change: The experience of the British Postal System," working technical paper, Department of Management Sciences, University of Manchester Institute of Science and Technology, UMIST, Manchester, UK, 1970.

Lowe, T. L. and J. F. Rounce, *Calculations for A-level Physics*, 4th ed., Nelson Thornes, Cheltenham, United Kingdom, 2002.

Mitiguy, Paul and Michael Woo, *Interactive Physics Curriculum Workbook*, Instructor Edition, Design Simulation Technologies, Canton, MI, 2006.

Nag, Pranab Kumar, "Maximal oxygen uptake of agricultural men and women in India," *American Journal of Physical Anthropology*, Volume 74, Issue 2, Pages149–153, 1987.

Peacock, John Brian, "The Physical Workload Involved in Parcel Handling," *Ergonomics*, Volume 23, No. 4, pp. 417–424, 1980.

SFC, *Saint Finbarr's College High School Physics Workbook*, Saint Finbarr's College, Akoka, Yaba, Nigeria, 1972.

Chapter 11
Soccer Trivia

The shape of a soccer ball is an example of a solid spherical polyhedron,[32] called a *truncated icosahedron*, which has twelve black pentagons, twenty white hexagons, sixty vertices, and ninety edges. The basic soccer ball design is shown in Figure 11.1.

Figure 11.1: Soccer ball shapes: solid spherical polyhedron

The ball consists of the same pattern of regular pentagons and regular hexagons, but is more spherical due to the pressure of the air inside and the elasticity of the ball. The polyhedron can be constructed from an icosahedron with the twelve vertices truncated (cut off) such that one third of each edge is cut off at each of both ends. This creates twelve new pentagon faces and leaves the original twenty triangle faces as regular hexagons. Thus, the length of the edges is one third that of the original edges. The area A and the volume V of the truncated icosahedron with edge length a are calculated as shown in the equation below:

$$A = 3\left(10\sqrt{3} + \sqrt{5}\sqrt{5 + 2\sqrt{5}}\right)a^2 \approx 72.607253a^2$$

$$V = \frac{1}{4}\left(125 + 43\sqrt{5}\right)a^3 \approx 55.2877308a^3$$

Some interesting trivial[33] pieces of soccer information include the following:

---

32. www.soccersaurus.com/infosoccertriviaandfacts.html
33. ezinearticles.com/?Soccer-Trivia-and-Facts&id=200678

- Soccer originated generally in its present form in Britain.
- The world's oldest club, formed in 1857, is Sheffield FC.
- Soccer is the most played and most watched sport on Earth.
- Soccer is called football in practically every country except the United States, where it is called soccer.
- Famous soccer rivalries include the Old Firm (Scotland), Manchester derby, London derbies, Milan derby, Real versus Barcelona, and many more. Note that derbies are matches between pro teams from the same city. They usually lead to intra-city rivalries.
- Danny Blanchflower was a famous Irish footballer. Once he was asked by a journalist why he thought that his team had just won an important match. He thought a while and then responded, "Perhaps it was because we scored more goals than the other side." His modern counterpart would have said emphatically: "Because the other side scored less than we did."
- Famous soccer players include Pele, Maradona, Charlton, Eusebio, Cruyff, Dalglish, Ronaldo, Beckham, and Mattheus.
- Soccer is the most popular team sport in the world, in both number of spectators and number of active participants.
- The largest attendance ever recorded for a soccer match was 199,854 people: Brazil v. Uruguay in the World Cup at the Maracana Municipal Stadium, Rio de Janeiro, July 1950.
- In the largest soccer tournament ever, no less than 5,098 teams competed in 1999 for the second Bangkok League Seven-a-Side Competition, with over 35,000 players involved.
- The most goals scored by one player in a single major soccer match was sixteen by Stephan Stanis (France) playing for Racing Club de Lens in December 1942.
- Based on video evidence, one of the fastest goals ever scored was 2.8 seconds by Ricardo Olivera (Uruguay) in December 1998.
- The international governing body of soccer is the *Federation Internationale de Football Association* (FIFA), based in Zurich, Switzerland.

- Diego Maradona was only sixteen when he made his soccer debut for Argentina.
- Soccer goalies didn't have to wear different colored shirts from their teammates until 1913.
- Eusebio scored forty-six goals in the European Cup for Benfica.
- Chris Woods once went 1,196 minutes without conceding a goal while at Rangers, from between November 26, 1986, and January 31, 1987.
- In 1973, the entire Galilee team spent the night in jail for kicking their opponents during an Israeli League game.

Author's Soccer Heritage

The author comes from a rich heritage of the game of soccer. He grew up in Lagos, Nigeria, a soccer-crazy country on the west coast of Africa. The principal of the high school was the famous Irish Catholic priest, Reverend Father Denis J. Slattery, who served multiple purposes at the school as teacher, preacher, soccer coach, and referee. While at the school, the author played on the junior-level teams designed to prepare boys for the full-fledged first-eleven team later on. Although he was a decent player, he was never fully committed to being on the regular team of Saint Finbarr's College. The competition for securing a spot on the regular school team, which would be called the varsity team in America, was incredibly keen, but the author wasn't fully committed to training to be a regular soccer player. Saint Finbarr's College football players were of a different stock: highly skilled and talented. Many of them, even in high school, could have played on professional teams. In later years, recalling his Saint Finbarr's soccer heritage, the author did blossom into a more respectable recreational player. He played on his university team at Tennessee Technological University in Cookeville, Tennessee, in 1977, and later on adult recreational teams in Florida, Oklahoma, and Tennessee. The photo in Figure 11.2 shows the author on the Tennessee Tech University soccer team in Cookeville in 1977.

Figure 11.2: Tennessee Tech University Soccer Team, 1977

Soccer at Saint Finbarr's College

The seed for writing this sort of book was planted in the mind of the author while at Saint Finbarr's College, where the principal, Reverend Father Denis J. Slattery, insisted on combining high-level academics with soccer excellence. In fact, the high school was most noted for three characteristics:

1. Academics

2. Soccer

3. Discipline

These three elements of the author's soccer heritage form the integral platform for writing this book to combine the science of physics, soccer skills development, and player self-discipline. The school's old game song went something like this:

> "Finbarr's is winning today, Finbarr's is winning,
> Finbarr's is winning, Finbarr's is winning today ...
> You can go to England and bring Bobby Charleton,

Finbarr's is winning today. Play the game for fun
and love of the game."

The above song, indeed, sets the tone to having fun with soccer. The photo collage in Figure 11.3 shows Father Slattery in different soccer roles as soccer administrator, coach, and referee.

Figure 11.3: Saint Finbarr's College soccer images

Chapter 12
Scientific Management of Soccer

Soccer game management is as important as any other field of management in business or industry. The concepts of scientific management are also applicable to managing a soccer team. As a soccer coach–player in the early 1990s, the author applied his professional management skills to developing a process for total game management on and off the soccer playing field. Management principles and discipline instilled by the technique of total quality management (TQM) can be used to improve any process ranging from recreational activities to professional endeavors.

Management skills are very essential for achieving success in all facets of the game of soccer. The best technically capable coaches have been known to fail due to poor leadership abilities and inadequate management skills. There are many highly placed managers whose technical skills far exceed their leadership capabilities. This brings to mind the **Peter Principle** of management which says that "people tend to be promoted to their level of incompetence," whereby they do not have inherent management skills needed to perform well (Badiru et al 2008). The Triple C model presented by Badiru (2008) offers useful guidelines for effective communication, cooperation, and coordination to get the best performance out of a team.

Concept of Six Sigma

In the business world, "lean," Six Sigma, and project management concepts (Badiru and Ayeni 1993, Badiru 1995, Badiru 2009) are used to improve processes and procedures for accomplishing work. These same concepts can be applied to the business of soccer management. Training management, game execution management, and soccer organization management can benefit from lean and Six Sigma techniques.

The Six Sigma approach, which was originally introduced by Motorola's Government Electronics Group,[34] has caught on quickly in business and industry. Many major companies now embrace the approach as the key to high-quality business productivity. *Six Sigma* means six standard deviations from a statistical performance average (Furterer 2009, Gitlow 2009). The Six Sigma approach allows for no

---

34.   www.highbeam.com/doc/1G1-149769621.html

more than 3.4 defects per million parts in manufactured goods or 3.4 mistakes per million activities in a service operation. To appreciate the effect of the Six Sigma approach, consider a process that is 99 percent perfect. That process will produce 10,000 defects per million parts. With Six Sigma, the process will need to be 99.99966 percent perfect in order to produce only 3.4 defects per million. Thus, Six Sigma is an approach that pushes the limit of perfection. The technique of Six Sigma (Badiru and Ayeni 1993) uses statistical methods to find problems that cause defects so that they can be corrected. For example, the total yield (number of nondefective units) from a process is determined by a combination of the performance levels of all the steps making up the process. If a process consists of twenty steps, and each step is 98 percent correct, then the overall fidelity of the composite process is:

$$(0.98)^{20} = 0.667608 \text{ (i.e., 66.7608\%)}$$

Thus, the process will produce 332,392 defects per million parts. If each step of the process is pushed to the Six Sigma limit, then the process performance will have the following composite performance level:

$$(0.9999966)^{20} = 0.999932 \text{ (i.e., 99.9932\%)}$$

Based on the above calculation, the Six Sigma process will produce only 68 defects per million parts. This is a significant improvement over the original process performance. In many cases, it is not realistic to expect to achieve the Six Sigma level of production. But the approach helps to set a quality standard and provides a mechanism for striving to reach the target goal. In effect, the Six Sigma process means changing the way workers perform their tasks so as to minimize the potential for defects.

Concept of Lean Process

What is *lean*? Lean, in the context of industrial processes (Badiru et al. 2008), means the identification and elimination of sources of *waste* in operations. Six Sigma involves the identification and elimination of sources of *defects* (Gitlow 2009, Furterer 2009). When lean and Six Sigma are combined (known as *lean Six Sigma*), an organization can reduce both waste and defects in operations. Consequently, the organization can achieve higher product quality, better employee morale, more satisfied customers, and more effective utilization of limited resources. The basic principle of lean is to take a close look at the elemental compositions of a process to eliminate non-value-adding elements (or movements). Lean and Six Sigma techniques use analytical and statistical techniques as the basis for pursuing improvement objectives. But the achievement of those goals depends on having a structured approach to the activities associated with what needs to be done.

If proper project management is embraced at the outset in a soccer management endeavor, it will pave the way for achieving Six Sigma results and make it possible to realize lean outcomes. The key in any soccer management endeavor is to have a structured plan so that diagnostic and corrective steps can be pursued. If the proverbial "garbage" is allowed to creep into a soccer effort, it would take much more time, effort, and cost to achieve a lean Six Sigma cleanup.

To put the above concepts in a soccer perspective, Six Sigma implies conducting soccer practice such that errors are minimized in the long run. Likewise, the technique of lean ensures that only value-adding movements are made during practice and games. For example, the ability to pass the ball within close quarters on the soccer field is highly coveted and requires hours and hours of practice. When it becomes like second nature, it can be done intuitively. An analogy for lean Six Sigma application to soccer movement is illustrated in Figure 12.1. If practice involves moving the ball within close confines, then Six Sigma means the ability to consistently keep the ball within specification (specs) limits. Balls falling outside specs limits do not meet "quality" requirements. That means they fall outside specs. In applying a lean concept approach, being able to keep the ball close means avoiding unnecessary motions. This means the elimination of waste. This brings to mind ***Parkinson's Law*** of bureaucracy, which states that "work expands to fill the time available," as a result of which unnecessary activities are performed (Badiru et al 2008).

Coaches must ensure that practice does not extend needlessly just to use up available time. Short and effective routines are better than protracted ones that result in counterproductive results.

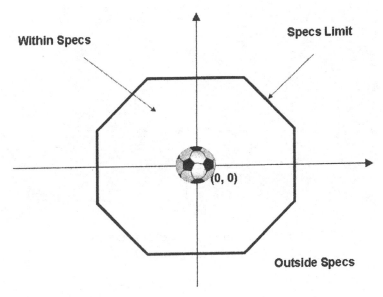

Figure 12.1: Movement control limits for practice area

Case Study of Practical Application of Management

Case studies are a good approach for learning the applications of management techniques (Furterer 2009). The author has a personal case study experience in the application of the concepts of TQM process in coaching a soccer team. The author became the coach of an adult recreational soccer team in fall 1992 in the Central Oklahoma Adult Soccer League. The 1994 team is shown in Figure 12.2. Using TQM processes, he took the team from being at the bottom of the league to being the league champion in just three seasons. This was not due to his coaching acumen, but rather, the way he motivated the team and made everyone aware of their respective responsibilities on the team on and off the field.

Figure 12.2: Author on adult soccer team,
Norman, Oklahoma, 1994

The greatest risk to losing an adult recreational soccer game is players not showing up. This was in an "over-thirty" league, stylishly referred to as the Masters League, where most of the players were technical or business professionals. Life, at the age of the Masters, is full of competing priorities. Several times, we had to smuggle a starting player out of his house, out of sight of his disapproving wife. When caught in the act, a typical conversation might be as follows:

> *Star's spouse:* "What do you guys think you are do-ing?"
> *Teammate:* "We are here to pick up Emmanuel for a weekend meeting at work."
> *Star's spouse:* "Oh yeah?"
> *Teammate:* "Yeah! The boss wants everyone there. It's a strategic planning weekend retreat."
> *Star's spouse:* "So, why is he stuffing extra-strength Ben-gay cream in his coat pocket?"
> *Teammate:* "It's one of those management games where co-workers use physical contacts for team

building exercises. Don't worry, we'll have him back intact in a couple of hours."

At this point, everyone would burst out laughing while the team car, full of crouching adults, zoomed off. As comedian Woody Allen said, "Eighty percent of success is showing up."

The team could not afford for any player not to show up. So, management trickery and covert operations were often needed to get players to the games.

As a coach-player, the author applied TQM techniques to the way he handled team assignments and encouraged the other players to do likewise. He developed a documentation system that, each week, informed the players of where the team stood in relation to other teams. Each week, he handed out written notes about what the current objectives were and how they would be addressed. Because of this, he was nicknamed the "Memo Coach." It got to a point where the players got used to being given written assignments, and they would jokingly demand their memo for the week. Copies of graphical representations of the game lineup were given to the players to study prior to each game. Each person had to know his immediate coordination points during a game: who would provide support for whom, who would cover what area of the field, and so on. He applied TQM to various aspects of the team including the following:

- Team registration
- Team motivation
- Team communication
- Team cooperation
- Team coordination
- Expected individual commitment
- Player camaraderie
- Field preparation
- Sportsmanship
- Play etiquette
- Game lineup
- Training regimen
- Funding

Everybody had an assignment that was explained and coordinated for total team and game management. In the second season under this unconventional coach, the team took third place. The players were all excited and motivated and credited the success to the way the management of the team was handled. So, starting the third season, everyone came out highly charged up to move the team forward to an even better season. Of course, there was the season's inaugural memo waiting for the team.

One of the favorite memos handed out to the team was the one that indicated the team's record (Win-Lose-Draw) dating back ten years. With this, the coach was able to motivate the team; it was time to move to the higher levels of the league. Traditionally, the team had been viewed as one of the "so-so" teams in the league. Not a bad team, but not among the best either. The coach convinced the players that while winning was not everything (particularly in an adult soccer league), it sure would feel better than losing.

With the high level of motivation, division of labor, and effective utilization of existing resources (soccer skills, or lack thereof), the team was crowned the league champion for fall 1993. This is not a small feat in a league with several powerhouses. It is interesting to note that the achievement was made with little or no recruitment of additional "skillful" players, who were in short supply anyway in that league at that time. This shows that with proper management, existing resources of a team can be leveraged to achieve an unprecedented level of improvement in direct skills development as well as total team and game management. In particular, using the techniques of project management for soccer management has many advantages, including the following:

- Better connection with other players
- Better lines of communication
- More sustainable levels of cooperation
- Better pathways of coordination
- Holistic systems view of soccer game scenarios

Don't Drop the Ball

Whether you are a player, coach, parent, referee, or league administrator, don't drop the ball when it comes to crucial affairs of soccer, as caricatured in Figure 12.3. Use total team management, as in total quality management, to avoid dropping the ball.

Figure 12.3: Steps of soccer practice, game plan, and game control

Health and Bodily Care

In order to excel at soccer, you must not only be skillful and in good shape, you must also be healthy. Take good care of your health. Eat right and sleep well. Avoid bumps and accidents that may impede your physical movements and prevent you from playing at the highest level. Make healthy personal choices, and you will remain healthy to execute your soccer game plans successfully. Make personal bad choices, and they will come back to haunt you during a game, particularly the very important ones like championship games. Poor health and a sour outlook impede the ability to play effectively.

Take care of yourself so that you can take care of your game. Avoid self-destructive lifestyles, such as bad posture, poor body mechanics, obesity, smoking, reckless driving, fast living, drug abuse, gambling, and poor diet.

Likewise, take responsibility to take care of your means of transportation to get to practice and games. Take care of your car so that you can get to where you need to be promptly to do what you need to do in a timely manner. Many games these days depend on accessible modes of transportation. Thus, game-play implementation can be very car-dependent. Getting to a game on time, arriving on time for practice, and reaching the soccer field safely can all be impacted by your vehicle's operational condition. For example, if you get your car ready for winter driving conditions, you will experience fewer car-related delays. Winter transportation problems can be preempted by doing the following:

- Service and maintain radiator system.
- Replace windshield-wiper fluid with appropriate winter mixture.
- Check tire pressure regularly.
- Replace worn tires.
- Maintain a full tank of fuel during winter months to keep ice from forming in the tank and fuel lines.
- Have ice scrapers accessible within passenger space in the vehicle, not stored in the trunk.

Use of Self-Regulation

Have you ever considered yourself as a resource for your team? That is, a resource that should be managed and regulated? Taking care of yourself is a direct example of human resource management, which is crucial for soccer game success. Proper diet, exercise, and sleep are essential for mental alertness and positively impact the ability to get things done. Sleep, for example, affects many aspects of mental and physical activities. Sleep more and you will be amazed that you can get your soccer game to the next level. This is because being well-rested translates to making fewer errors. The notion that you have to stay up to get more done is not necessarily always true. Likewise, keep fit and advance your soccer game.

Game Ball Award

The game ball award is to be voted by coaches and teammates; to receive a championship game ball or sportsmanship award is a reflection of being a total person rather than just being a good soccer player. This is a much-cherished recognition that should be celebrated.

Etiquette Guide for Special Interest Groups

"There's a lot of things going on, a lot of different agendas with people playing different cards that I just can't fight without it hurting the kids."

—Bill Slagle, Springfield (Ohio) High School basketball coach, during his resignation from the coaching job

If it weren't for parents, I'd still be coaching youth soccer. Parents and coaches often have irreconcilable differences. In some cases, the coach must protect young players from the acts of their parents. Parents sometimes become the hooligans of youth soccer. Parents have undergone a transformation over the years. They have gone from discouraging kids from playing, either because they needed them to do "real" work on the farm or because of safety concerns, to excessive encouragement. Some special interest groups erroneously perceive youth sport as possessing the potential for sports contracts and riches later on (even if the players don't have the inherent abilities to achieve those heights). Special interest groups should step aside and let youth enjoy their sport, thrive, and advance with the sport.

Play the Game, Don't Play the Foul

During the 2009 NBA Finals, the coach of the Orlando Magic, Stan Van Gundy, was widely harangued because he did not order his team to foul the Lakers. Rather than criticize him, this author viewed him as a hero. Whatever happened to sportsmanship? When growing up, the author was coached to play fair and focus on outdoing opponents through skillful play rather than fouling. The criticism of Van Gundy is symptomatic of how society has degenerated. The concern is that those ranting about Van Gundy's foul failure would not bat an eye on fouling ethics to get ahead in life. It seems that we have thrown out the time-honored phrase of "May the better team win," and we now seem to embrace "May the foulest team win." Thanks to sports decadence, kids now face the risk of growing up believing that the only way to create a winning edge is to elbow, pinch, kick, trip, or even bite opponents. This author offers an alternative: Play the game, don't play the foul.

The Problem of Fan Violence

It was reported in July 2009 that soccer fan violence in Brazil kills about four people each year. In a study by Maurico Murad, a sociologist, deaths related to soccer games are also on the rise in Brazil, which is hosting the 2014 World Cup. Murad's data show that forty-two people were killed in connection with Brazilian soccer games in the last ten years. Argentina and Italy led the park with forty-nine and forty-five deaths, respectively, during the same period.

One of the most tragic soccer experiences was the brutal murder of Colombian soccer star, Andres Escobar, by a crazed fan in 1994 in retaliation for Escobar's inadvertent error of kicking the ball into his own team's goal. Soccer has become a major political, social, and economic force in many developing nations, where frustrated fans often express their disgust through senseless acts of violence, not only against opponents, but also against their own stars.

The 2010 World Cup is scheduled to be played in South Africa, and as of the time of this writing, there is still an opportunity to take preemptive steps to curb fan violence at the games. The general call is for nations to pass laws specifically targeting strategies to stem soccer violence. The physics of it all is that opposing groups collide with equal and opposite forces, and once the damage is done, it is irrecoverable.

Success Examples

The newspaper clippings and graphics in this section document the author's success in applying scientific and management principles in this book to recreational soccer as a youth soccer coach and adult coach-player in the mid-1990s. Figure 12.4 shows his award plaque for coaching.

Figure 12.4: Image of coach's award plaque

==

The Norman (Okla.) Transcript, Tuesday, May 6, 1997

Dragons undefeated

Monroe Dragons 6 COED soccer team went undefeated during spring regular season play with a 7-0 record. The team beat regular-season opponents by a margin of 84-25. Team members include Tunji Badiru, Scott Hanna-Riggs, Hunter Madole, Blake Smith, Nick Suit, and Chelsey Womack. The team is coached by Deji Badiru. (The team is shown in Figure 12.5.)

Figure 12.5: 1997 Monroe elementary soccer team
coached by author

===

The Norman (Okla.) Transcript, Thursday, October 6, 1994

Crusaders impale Impact

The Norman Crusaders defeated the Oklahoma City Impact last weekend in Central Oklahoma Adult Soccer League action at Whittier Middle School. David Morse scored two goals and Ernie Terrell, Emmanuel Akande and John Masango each had one. David Bolfrey dished out two assists and Miguel Grijalva had one assist and played steady defense in support of goalkeepers Craig Nelson and Chris Lajuwomi. The Crusaders, now 4-0, play defending state champion, Oklahoma City Soccer Center, Sunday at MacFarland Park. The Crusaders are coached by coach-player Deji Badiru.

===

The Norman (Okla.) Transcript, Friday, October 14, 1994

Crusaders tie state champs

The Norman Crusaders tied the defending state champion Soccer Center 3-3 Sunday at MacFarland Park in the Central Oklahoma Adult Soccer League. David Bolfrey and John Nash Masango scored goals.

===

The Norman (Okla.) Transcript, Friday, October 18, 1994

Crusaders still unbeaten

The Norman Crusaders defeated the Oklahoma City Intruders 6-1 Sunday in Central Oklahoma Adult Soccer League action at Whittier Middle School. John Nash Masango scored two goals and Ade Okewole, David Morse, David Bolfrey and Miguel Grijalva also scored for the Crusaders, 5-0-1. Bolfrey and Ernie Terrel had assists while Emmanuel Akande, Mike Tonubbee and Manuel Aguilar provide stout defense to support Craig Nelson's goaltending. Crusaders coach is Deji Badiru.

===

Crusaders scald City Heat

The Norman Crusaders defeated City Heat 4-1 last weekend in Central Oklahoma Adult Soccer League play at Whittier Middle School. David Bolfrey scored two goals and Ernie Terrel and Randy Venk each scored one. Deji Badiru had an assist while Craig Nelson and Nash Masango shared time as goalkeepers. Bob Byers, Ed Bonzie, Miguel Grijalva and Al Larsen also turned in strong play for the Crusaders, 6-0-1.

===

Crusaders trim Vista

The Norman Crusaders Soccer Club defeated Vista 4-1 last weekend in Central Oklahoma Adult Soccer League play at Whittier Middle School. Ade Okewole scored two goals for the Crusaders, now 7-0-1. Nash Masango and Ed Bonzie each scored one. Doug Reimer turned in a solid performance both as sweeper and back-up goalie for Craig Nelson. Mike Tonubbee, Manny Aguilar, Miguel Grijalva and Emmanuel Akande played strong defense. Deji Badiru is coach-player for the Crusaders.

===

Crusaders claim title

The Norman Crusaders defeated Soccer Center 6-3 Sunday to capture the Central Oklahoma Adult Soccer League Title for the second time in three years. David Bolfrey and Ade Okewole each scored two goals and Ernie Terrell and Emmanuel Akande each had one goal. Molua Lambe, Chris Lajuwomi, David Morse and Nash

Masango contributed assists for the Crusaders (8-0-1), who had been tied earlier in the season by Soccer Center. Akande, Manuel Aguilar, Mike Tonubbee and Doug Reimer played solid defense while Ed Bonzie, Bob Byers, Miguel Grijalva, Randy Venk and coach-player Deji Badiru excelled at midfield. Goalie Craig Nelson added several spectacular saves.

(For his contributions to the championship title, the author was given the award certificate shown in Figure 12.6.)

==

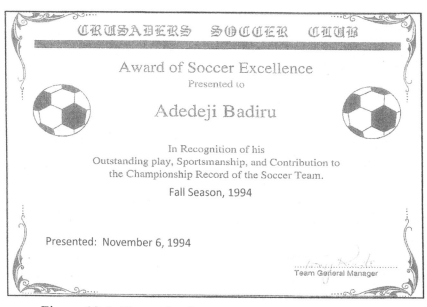

Figure 12.6: The author's soccer award certificate, 1994

==

The Norman (Okla.) Transcript, Thursday, March 16, 1995

Crusaders open with win

The Norman Crusaders adult soccer team opened the season with an 11-0 victory over Impact. Brent Maze and Nash Masango scored three goals, Ernie Terrell scored two and Ade Okewole, Shelly

Lambe and Miguel Grijalva each scored once. Jim Rice, Emmanuel Akande played solid defense and Craig Nelson posted the shutout. The team is coached by Deji Badiru.

The Norman (Okla.) Transcript, Tuesday, March 28, 1995

Crusaders cool off Heat

The Norman Crusaders defeated City Heat 4-2 Sunday in Central Oklahoma Adult Soccer League play. Ernie Terrell scored two goals. Ade Okewole and David Bolfrey each scored one goal. Emmanuel Akande, Jim Rice, Mike Tonubbee, Manny Aguilar and goalie Craig Nelson paced the defense for Coach-player Deji Badiru's Crusaders.

The Norman (Okla.) Transcript, Thursday, April 6, 1995

Crusaders edge Liberty

The Norman Crusaders defeated Liberty 4-2 Sunday in Central Oklahoma Adult Soccer League play. Nash Masango scored two goals while Brent Maze and Reza Khakpour each tallied once. David Bolfrey and Ade Okewole each had an assist. Shelly Lambe, Ernie Terrell and David Morse played strong on defense. Emmanuel Akande, Manny Aguilar, Mike Tonubbee, Randy Venk, Doug Reimer and Miguel Grijalva shined on defense and goalie Craig Nelson made several spectacular saves to preserve the win. The Crusaders, the defending season champs, are coached by Deji Badiru.

Crusaders dump Intruders

The Norman Crusaders defeated the Intruders 5-2 Sunday in Central Oklahoma Adult Soccer League action. Pato Morales, Shelly Lambe, Chris Lajuwomi, Reza Khakpour and David Morse scored goals for the Crusaders. Ade Okewole had two assists. Coach-player Deji Badiru, Miguel Grijalva, Randy Venk, Al Larsen, Nash Masango, Ernie Terrell, Jim Rice and goalie Craig Nelson also played well.

===

Well, to prove that everything good comes to an end, eventually, the championship reign of the Crusaders adult soccer team came to an end in May 1995, as documented by the league's news account below:

"The Norman Crusaders Soccer Club lost 2-4 to Pyramid Soccer Club on Sunday, May 14 in the season play-offs of the Central Oklahoma Adult Soccer League. Coach-player Deji Badiru and Ade Okewole each scored one goal for the Crusaders. Emmanuel Akande, Jim Rice, Manny Aguilar, and Mike Tonubbee played hard on defense. Ernie Terrell, David Morse, Pato Morales, Reza Khakpour, Bob Byers, Miguel Grijalva, Al Larsen and Pato Morales all played very strong. Craig Nelson played strong in goal. The play-off games continue Sunday at North Oklahoma City Soccer Complex."

Chapter 12 References

Badiru, Adedeji B., *STEP Project Management: Guide for Science, Technology, and Engineering Projects*, Taylor & Francis/CRC Press, Boca Raton, FL, 2009.

Badiru, Adedeji B., *Triple C Model of Project Management: Communication, Cooperation, and Coordination*, Taylor & Francis CRC Press, Boca Raton, FL, 2008.

Badiru, Adedeji B., *Industry's Guide to ISO 9000*, John Wiley & Sons, New York, NY, 1995.

Badiru, Adedeji B., Abi Badiru, and Ade Badiru, *Industrial Project Management: Concepts, Tools, and Techniques*, Taylor & Francis/ CRC Press, Boca Raton, FL, 2008.

Badiru, Adedeji B. and B. J. Ayeni, *Practitioner's Guide to Quality and Process Improvement*, Chapman & Hall, London, 1993.

Furterer, Sandra L. (Ed.), *Lean Six Sigma in Service: Applications and Case Studies*, Taylor & Francis/CRC Press, Boca Raton, FL, 2009.

Gitlow, Howard S., *A Guide to Lean Six Sigma Management Skills*, Taylor & Francis/CRC Press, Boca Raton, FL, 2009.

Epilogue

The Physics of Soccer: Using Math and Science to Improve Your Game provides fascinating and wide-ranging topics of science, technology, engineering, and mathematics (STEM) from the perspective of applying them to the game of soccer. Although the main focus is the application of physics to soccer, several managerial issues are also addressed in the book. The game of soccer, as it is played physically on the field, should take advantage of the intellectual tools, knowledge, and techniques of STEM. This book plays a role in that goal. Knowing more about the physics behind the game of soccer will enable players to approach the game more from an intellectual viewpoint rather than just from the physical standpoint. The main tenet of the book entails the following:

- Viewing the game from an intellectual point of view
- Using mathematical and scientific reasoning to improve game performance
- Using brains rather than brawn to gain an edge over opponents

The Physics of Soccer will whet the appetite of young players for the application of math and science to improve their performance and excel at soccer.

Appendix
Units of Measure and Conversion Factors

Significant Figures

The level of accuracy desired and the associated value often determine the measurement tool, approach, and units. In order to describe the accuracy of a single measurement, it can be presented in terms of a set of significant figures. A significant figure in a number can be defined as a figure that may be considered reliable as a result of measurement or due to the mathematical computations. For example, a soccer kick that is estimated as coming from 18.5 yards outside the box indicates three significant figures if expressed as 1.85×10^1. The "5" is significant in this case because on the soccer field, half of a yard (0.5 yard) could be significant enough in terms of the accuracy between the soccer ball crossing the goal line or not crossing it.

Scientific Notation

The decimal point has nothing to do with how many significant figures there are in a measured number. It is the inherent level of accuracy associated with the number that matters. For example, it is impossible to tell the number of significant figures if a number is written as 123,000 or 123000 in a measured datum. To ascertain the number of significant figures, use the following rules:

1. Move the decimal point to the left or right until a number between 1 and 10 remains. The number that results from this process contains only significant figures.

2. The remaining number must now be multiplied by a power of ten. That is, (10) raised to an exponent representing the number of decimal moves.

Suppose we desire to express the number 123,000 to three significant figures. Applying the above rules, we have:

$$123,000 = 1.23 \times 10^5$$

Similarly, 0.0123000 expressed to three significant figures yields:

$$0.0123000 = 1.23 \times 10^{-2}$$

Likewise, the same number 0.0123000 expressed to five significant figures yields:

$$0.0123000 = 1.2300 \times 10^{-2}$$

Soccer field measurement accuracy can become crucial by inches in certain setups for free kicks (direct or indirect). Many soccer spectators have witnessed cases where the referee, using rudimentary foot-pace ten-yard measurement, had to physically move the defending line back, only to have the defender inch back as soon as he turns his back, while the shooting team mounts a vocal finger-pointing protest. This is a great example of significant digits of distance measurement and conversion.

Engineering Notation

From the conventional decimal notation and scientific notation, we now consider the engineering notation. The engineering notation complements the increasing popularity of the metric system of measurement. The underlying concept of the engineering notation is that quantities are to be specified so that the exponents of 10 are always equally divisible by 3. This implies that the exponents of 10 will have values of $3 \pm n(3)$, where n is an integer; which yields the numbers ...., -12, -9, -6, -3, 0, +3, +6, +9, +12, ... This series of numbers fits in nicely with the common computer-oriented prefixes of:

pico, nano, micro, milli, kilo, mega, giga, tera

Engineering notation is a version of the more general exponential notation. The general exponential notation does not restrict exponents to multiples of three. Exponential notation gets rid of zeros, and thus makes mathematical calculations easier because we can use addition to accomplish multiplication and subtraction to achieve division. Also, getting rid of zeros makes it easier to handle both large and small numbers. For example:

9,000,000 can be rewritten as 9×10^6
and
0.000009 can be rewritten as 9×10^{-6}

To express a quantity in engineering notation requires selecting a value between 1 and less than 1,000 (i.e., $1 \leq$ value $< 1,000$), which, when multiplied by 10 raised to an exponent exactly divisible by 3, yields the desired quantity. The tables that follow present useful constants and conversion factors.

English system of measurement: Miles, yards, feet
Metric system of measurement: Kilometers

Table A.1: Notational conventions

Conventional notation	Scientific notation	Engineering notation
12,345.7	1.23457×10^4	12.3457×10^3
123.456	1.23456×10^2	123.456×10^0
20	2.0×10^1	20×10^0
0.675	6.75×10^{-1}	675×10^{-3}
0.0001	1×10^{-4}	100×10^{-6}

Table A.2: Exponential notations, prefixes, and expansions

Notation Expansion

Notation	Expansion
yotta (10^{24}):	1,000,000,000,000,000,000,000,000
zetta (10^{21}):	1,000,000,000,000,000,000,000
exa (10^{18}):	1,000,000,000,000,000,000
peta (10^{15}):	1,000,000,000,000,000
tera (10^{12}):	1,000,000,000,000
giga (10^{9}):	1,000,000,000
mega (10^{6}):	1,000,000
kilo (10^{3}):	1,000
hecto (10^{2}):	100
deca (10^{1}):	10
deci (10^{-1}):	0.1
centi (10^{-2}):	0.01
milli (10^{-3}):	0.001
micro (10^{-6}):	0.000001
nano (10^{-9}):	0.000000001
pico (10^{-12}):	0.000000000001
femto (10^{-15}):	0.000000000000001
atto (10^{-18}):	0.000000000000000001
zepto (10^{-21}):	0.000000000000000000001
yocto (10^{-24}):	0.000000000000000000000001
stringo (10^{-35}):	0.00000000000000000000000000000000001

Table A.3: English and metric systems of measurement

English system	
1 foot (ft)	= 12 inches (in) 1' = 12"
1 yard (yd)	= 3 feet
1 mile (mi)	= 1,760 yards
1 sq. foot	= 144 square inches
1 sq. yard	= 9 square feet
1 acre	= 4,840 square yards = 43,560 ft²
1 sq. mile	= 640 acres
Metric system	
mm	millimeter (0.001m)
cm	centimeter (0.01m)
dm	decimeter (0.1m)
m	meter (1m)
dam	decameter (10m)
hm	hectometer (100m)
km	kilometer (1,000m)

Table A.4: Common units of measurement

Measurement	Symbol	Description
meter	m	length
hectare	ha	area
tonne	t	mass
kilogram	kg	mass
nautical mile	M	distance (navigation)
knot	kn	speed (navigation)
liter	L	volume or capacity
second	s	time
hertz	Hz	frequency
candela	cd	luminous intensity
degree Celsius	°C	temperature
Kelvin	K	thermodynamic temp.
pascal	Pa	pressure, stress
joule	J	energy, work
newton	N	force
watt	W	power, radiant flux
ampere	A	electric current
volt	V	electric potential
ohm	Ω	electric resistance
coulomb	C	electric charge

Table A.5: Distance conversion factors

Multiply	by	to obtain
angstrom	10^{-10}	meters
feet	0.30480	meters
	12	inches
inches	25.40	millimeters
	0.02540	meters
	0.08333	feet
kilometers	3,280.8	feet
	0.6214	miles
	1,094	yards
meters	39.370	inches
	3.2808	feet
	1.094	yards
miles	5,280	feet
	1.6093	kilometers
	0.8694	nautical miles
millimeters	0.03937	inches
nautical miles	6,076	feet
	1.852	kilometers
yards	0.9144	meters
	3	feet
	36	inches

Table A.6: Velocity conversion factors

Multiply	by	to obtain
feet/minute	5.080	mm/second
feet/second	0.3048	meters/second
inches/second	0.0254	meters/second
km/hour	0.6214	miles/hour
meters/second	3.2808	feet/second
	2.237	miles/hour
miles/hour	88.0	feet/minute
	0.44704	meters/second
	1.6093	km/hour
	0.8684	knots
knot	1.151	miles/hour

Table A.7: Mass conversion factors

Multiply	by	to obtain
carat	0.200	cubic grams
grams	0.03527	ounces
kilograms	2.2046	pounds
ounces	28.350	grams
pound	16	ounces
	453.6	grams
stone (UK)	6.35	kilograms
	14	pounds
ton (net)	907.2	kilograms
	2,000	pounds
	0.893	gross ton
	0.907	metric ton
ton (gross)	2,240	pounds
	1.12	net tons
	1.016	metric tons
tonne (metric)	2,204.623	pounds
	0.984	gross pound
	1,000	kilograms

Table A.8: Area conversion factors

Multiply	by	to obtain
acres	43,560 4,047 4,840 0.405	sq feet sq meters sq yards hectare
sq cm	0.155	sq inches
sq feet	144 0.09290 0.1111	sq inches sq meters sq yards
sq inches	645.16	sq millimeters
sq kilometers	0.3861	sq miles
sq meters	10.764 1.196	sq feet sq yards
sq miles	640 2.590	acres sq kilometers

Table A.9: Volume conversion factors

Multiply	by	to obtain
acre-foot	1,233.5	cubic meters
cubic cm	0.06102	cubic inches
cubic feet	1,728	cubic inches
	7.480	gallons (U.S.)
	0.02832	cubic meters
	0.03704	cubic yards
liter	1.057	liquid quarts
	0.908	dry quarts
	61.024	cubic inches
gallons (U.S.)	231	cubic inches
	3.7854	liters
	4	quarts
	0.833	British gallons
	128	U.S. fluid ounces
quarts (U.S.)	0.9463	liters

Table A.10: Energy conversion factors

Multiply	by	to obtain
BTU	1,055.9	joules
	0.2520	kg-calories
watt-hour	3,600	joules
	3.409	BTU
HP (electric)	746	watts
BTU/second	1,055.9	watts
watt-second	1.00	joules

Table A.11: Temperature conversion factors

Conversion formulas	
Celsius to Kelvin	$K = C + 273.15$
Celsius to Fahrenheit	$F = (9/5)C + 32$
Fahrenheit to Celsius	$C = (5/9)(F - 32)$
Fahrenheit to Kelvin	$K = (5/9)(F + 459.67)$
Fahrenheit to Rankin	$R = F + 459.67$
Rankin to Kelvin	$K = (5/9)R$

Table A.12: Pressure conversion factors

Multiply	by	to obtain
atmospheres	1.01325	bars
	33.90	feet of water
	29.92	inches of mercury
	760.0	mm of mercury
bar	75.01	cm of mercury
	14.50	pounds/sq inch
dyne/sq cm	0.1	N/sq meter
newtons/sq cm	1.450	pounds/sq inch
pounds/sq inch	0.06805	atmospheres
	2.036	inches of mercury
	27.708	inches of water
	68.948	millibars
	51.72	mm of mercury

Table A.13: Science constants

Speed of light	2.997925×10^{10} cm/sec
	983.6×10^{6} ft/sec
	186,284 miles/sec
Velocity of sound	340.3 meters/sec
	1,116 ft/sec
Gravity (acceleration)	9.80665 m/sec squared
	32.174 ft/sec squared
	386.089 inches/sec squared

Table A.14: Household measurements

1 pinch	1/8 teaspoon or less
3 teaspoons	1 tablespoon
2 tablespoons	1/8 cup
4 tablespoons	1/4 cup
8 tablespoons	1/2 cup
12 tablespoons	3/4 cup
16 tablespoons	1 cup
5 tablespoons + 1 teaspoon	1/3 cup
4 oz	1/2 cup
8 oz	1 cup
16 oz	1 lb
1 oz	2 tablespoons fat or liquid
1 cup of liquid	1/2 pint
2 cups	1 pint
2 pints	1 quart
4 cup of liquid	1 quart
4 quarts	1 gallon
8 quarts	1 peck (such as apples, pears, etc.)
1 jigger	1½ fluid oz
1 jigger	3 tablespoons

Table A.15: Physical science equations

$$D = \frac{m}{V} \left(\frac{g}{cm^3} = \frac{kg}{m^3} \right)$$

D   density
m   mass
V   volume

$$P = \frac{W}{t}$$

P   power; W (watts)
W   work (J)
t   time (s)

$$d = v \cdot t$$

d   distance (m)
v   velocity (m/s)
t   time (s)

$$K.E. = \frac{1}{2} \cdot m \cdot v^2$$

K.E.   kinetic energy
m   mass (kg)
v   velocity (m/s)

$$a = \frac{vf - vi}{t}$$

a   acceleration (m/s²)
vf   final velocity (m/s)
vi   initial velocity (m/s)
t   time (s)

$$d = vit + \frac{1}{2}at^2$$

d   distance (m)
vi   initial velocity (m/s)
t   time (s)
a   acceleration (m/s²)

$$F = m \cdot a$$

F   net force N (newtons)
m   mass (kg)
a   acceleration (m/s²)

$$V = \frac{W}{Q}$$

V   electrical potential
difference V (volts)
W   work done (J)
Q   electric charge flowing (C)

$$Fg = \frac{G \cdot m_1 \cdot m_2}{d^2}, \left(G = 6.67 \times 10^{-1} \frac{N - m^2}{kg^2} \right)$$

Fg force of gravity (N)
G   universal gravitational constant
m_1, m_2 masses of the two objects (kg)
d   separation distance (m)

$$I = \frac{Q}{t}$$

I   electric current ampères
Q   electric charge flowing (C)
t   time (s)

$$W = V \cdot I \cdot t$$

W   electrical energy (J)
V   voltage (V)
I   current (A)
t   time (s)

$$P = V \cdot I$$

P   power (W)
V   voltage (V)
I   current (A)

$$p = m \cdot v$$

p   momentum (kg·m/s)

m   mass

v   velocity

$$W = F \cdot d$$

W   work (J = joules)

F   force (N)

d   distance (m)

$$H = c \cdot m \cdot \ddot{A}T$$

H   heat energy (J)

m   mass (kg)

ΔT change in temperature ($^{\circ}C$)

c   specific heat (J/Kg·$^{\circ}C$)

Table A.16: Quick reference summary of metric conversion

KILOMETER-MILE CONVERSION			
Kilometers	Miles	Miles	Kilometers
1	0.6	1	1.6
5	3.1	5	8.05
10	6.2	10	16.0
20	12.4	20	32.1
30	18.6	30	48.2
40	24.8	40	64.3
50	31.1	50	80.5
60	37.3	60	96.6
70	43.5	70	112.7
80	49.7	80	128.7
90	55.9	90	144.8
100	62.1	100	160.9
500	310.7	500	804.7
1,000	621.4	1,000	1,609.3

METRIC TABLES			
CAPACITY		AREA	
10 milliliters	= 1 centiliter	100 sq. millimeters	= 1 sq. centimeter
10 centiliters	= 1 deciliter	100 sq. centimeters	= 1 sq. decimeter
10 deciliters	= 1 liter	100 sq. decimeters	= 1 sq. meter
10 liters	= 1 dekaliter	100 sq. meters	(centare)
10 dekaliters	= 1 hectoliter	10,000 sq. meters	= 1 are
1,000 liters	= 1 kiloliter (stere)	100 hectares	= 1 hectare
			= 1 sq. kilometer
LENGTH		WEIGHT	
10 millimeters	= 1 centimeter (cm)	10 milligrams	= 1 centigram
10 centimeters	= 1 decimeter	10 centigrams	= 1 decigram
10 decimeters	= 1 meter (m)	10 decigrams	= 1 gram
10 meters	= 1 dekameter	1,000 grams	= 1 kilogram (kg)
100 meters	= 1 hectometer	100 kilograms	= 1 quintal
1,000 meters	= 1 kilometer	1,000 kilograms	= 1 metric ton

METRIC - U.S. WEIGHTS AND MEASURES			
DRY MEASURE		LONG MEASURE	
1 pint	= 0.550599 liter	1 inch	= 2.54 centimeters
1 quart	= 1.101197 liters	1 yard	= 0.914401 meter
1 peck	= 8.80958 liters	1 mile	= 1.609347 kilometers
1 bushed	= 0.35238 hectoliter		
LIQUID MEASURE		SQUARE MEASURE	
1 pint	= 0.473167 liter	1 sq. inch	6.4516 sq. centimeters
1 quart	= 0.946332 liter	1 sq. foot	9.29034 sq. decimeters
1 gallon	= 3.785329 liters	1 sq. yard	0.836131 sq. meter
		1 acre	0.40469 hectares
		1 sq. mile	2.59 sq. kilometers
		1 sq. mile	259 hectares
AVOIRDUPOIS MEASURE		CUBIC MEASURE	
1 ounce	= 28.349527 grams	1 cu. inch	= 16.3872 cu. centimeters
1 pound	= 0.453592 kilograms	1 cu. foot	= 0.028317 cu. meter
1 short ton	= 0.90718486 metric ton	1 cu. yard	= 0.76456 cu. meter
1 long ton	= 1.01604704 metric tons		

Summary of Useful Relationships

$$\sin\theta = \frac{b}{c} \qquad \csc\theta = \frac{c}{b}$$

$$\cos\theta = \frac{a}{c} \qquad \sec\theta = \frac{c}{a}$$

$$\tan\theta = \frac{b}{a} \qquad \cot\theta = \frac{a}{b}$$

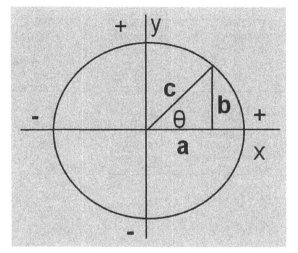

Figure A.1: Trigonometric relationships

1 radian	= 57.3°
1 inch	= 2.54 cm
1 gallon	= 231 in³
1 kilogram	= 2.205 lb
1 newton	= 1 kg • m/s²
1 joule	= 1 N • m
1 watt	= 1 J/s
1 pascal	= 1 N/m²
1 BTU	= 778 ft-lb
	= 252 cal
	= 1,054.8 J
1 horsepower	= 745.7 W
1 atmosphere	= 14.7 lb/in²
	= 1.01 • 10⁵ N/m²

Useful questions and answers

Question: How much does a gallon of gasoline weigh?
Answer: A gallon of gasoline weighs 5.93 lbs. to 6.42 lbs., or 2.69 kg to 2.91 kg, depending on temperature, type, and blend of gasoline (e.g., with methanol, water, benzene, gasohol, etc.).

Question: How much does a gallon of diesel weigh?
Answer: A gallon of diesel weighs approximately 7.3 lbs. (i.e., 0.9 kg/liter). The actual weight of diesel (or any other liquid) will vary slightly based on factors such as the exact chemical composition, temperature, gravity, additives, etc.

Question: How much does a gallon of water weigh?
Answer: A U.S. gallon of water weighs approximately 8.35 lbs. By comparison, the weight of 1 imperial gallon (UK measure) of water weighs 10 lbs. by definition, at a specified temperature and pressure.

Question: How much does a gallon of 15-weight motor oil weigh?
Answer: 1 gallon of oil weighs 7.344 lbs.

Question: How much does a gallon of 30-weight motor oil weigh?
Answer: 1 gallon of oil weighs 6.8 lbs.

Question: What is normal body temperature?
Answer: 98.6°F or 37.0°C

Index

Page numbers in *italics* refer to figures

cones, 184–87, 197, 199, 204
conjectures, in science, 13
conservation, of linear momentum, 150–51
constants, in physics, 36, *274*
constraints, in matches, 60
contact forces, 110–11
contact lenses, 87
conversion, of energy, 34
conversion, of measurements. *See also* scientific notation
    area, *271*
    distance, *268*
    energy, *273*
    importance of, 26–28
    mass, *270*
    metric vs. English, *28*, 264, *266*, *280–81*
    pressure, *274*
    temperature, *273*
    velocity, *269*
    volume, *272*
    weight, *281*
cornea, of eye, 84–85, *85*
corner kicks, 69, *95*, *98*
corns, on feet, 160
crooked line illusion, 132, *132*
Cross, Candi, xix
crowd control, 57
curving, of ball's trajectory. *See* bending, of ball's trajectory

D

dangerous play, signal for, *99*
Dayton Regional STEM School, 5–6
deceleration, 196
deception, 202. *See also* fake movements
decisions, rules and, 211
defect rates, in manufacturing, 238–39
defenders, 76, *78*
defensive play, 125–26, *180*, 207
dehydration, 192–93
density, 117
depth perception, 133–34

derbies, defined, 233
derivative, of function, 139
diet, 189–94
differential equations, 16
differentiation, in calculus, 139
dimensions
    of balls, 61
    of playing fields, *73*, *171*
direct free kicks, 69–71, 72, *94*
distance
    conversion tables, *268*
    measurement of, 263
    perception and, 133–34, 182–83
    in shooting, 203
    traveled over time, 135–36
distorting illusions, 132–33, *132–33*
diversity, of skills, 199–201
documentation systems, 243
drag, 16–17, 144–47
dribbling
    as ball control skill, 58
    described, 63, *63*, *80*, *90*
    on-the-run ball control, 81, *82*
    vs. passing, 206
    practice exercises, 185–86
    straddling and, 82, *83*

E

ears, 87–89, *88*
eating habits, 189–94
efficiency
    in physics, 10, 39
    in soccer, 189
effort, force of, 38–39
effort arm, of lever, 40
Egypt, tool use in, 39
Einstein, Albert, 24, 78
ejection, from game, 72, 93, *95*
electricity, 25, 32
electromagnetism, 25, 32
elephant's feet illusion, *131*
energy. *See also* physiological energy/work
    conversion tables, *273*
    distance and, 36–37

M

MA. *See* mechanical advantage (MA)
machines. *See also* technology
  inclined planes, 45–46, *45–46*
  levers, 39–42, *40–42*
  overview, 38–39
  pulleys, 44–45, *45*
  screws, 48
  wedges, 46–47, *47*
  wheels and axles, 42–43, *43*
Madole, Hunter, 250
magnetism, 25
Magnus, Heinrich, 118
Magnus force, 118–19, *119*
Major League Soccer (MLS) teams,
  7, *8*
management principles, 238–41
man-to-man marking, *172*
Maradona, Diego, 234
Mars orbiter, 26–27
Masango, John Nash, 251, 252, 253,
  254, 255, 256
mass
  conversion tables, *270*
  in physics, 111–12, 116, 117
  in soccer, 143–44
matches, generally, 59–60, 62, 193
mathematics, in STEM educational
  approach, 15–16
Mathews, Stanley, 199–200
maximum/minimum points, 138–41,
  140
Maya tribe, 54
Maze, Brent, 254, 255
measurements. *See also* conversion, of
  measurements
  common units, *267*
  household, *275*
  notation systems for, 26–28,
    263–64
  of physiological work, 190–94
mechanical advantage (MA)
  described, 38–39
  of machines, 43, 44, 45, 47, 48

mechanical energy, 32–33
mechanics. *See* kinematics
"Memo Coach," 243
metabolism. *See* physiological energy
metric measures, *28*, 264, *266*, *280–81*
Mexico, 54
midfielders, 74–75, 76, 126
midfoot, 157
minimum/maximum points, 138–41,
  140
misconduct. *See* fouls
mistakes, in manufacturing, 238–39
MLS teams, 7, *8*
mobility skills, overview, 59
momentum
  linear, 147
  player attributes and, 152–53
Monroe Dragons soccer team, 250–51,
  251
Morales, Pato, 256
Morse, David, 251, 252, 253, 255, 256
motion
  in physics, 108, 110–12, *176*
  in soccer, 78, *79*, 240
motivation, 192, 193, 199, 243, 244
Motorola Government Electronics
  Group, 238
moveable pulleys, 44
movement. *See* motion
Mullenax, Donna, xix
Murad, Maurico, 248
muscles. *See also* stamina; strength
  building
  of feet, 157
  geometry and, 179–80
myopia, 86

N

National Aeronautics and Space
  Administration (NASA), 26–27
Nelson, Craig, 252, 253, 254, 255, 256
Newton's laws of motion, 110–12
newton units, 111, 117
Nigerian soccer teams, 56, 113–14
Nintendo game systems, 6

Norman Crusaders soccer team, 241–44, *242*, 250–57
Norman Transcript clippings, 250–57
notational conventions, 262–65, *264*
novice swimmer syndrome, 10
nuclear energy, 33
nutrition, 189–94

O

Obama, Barack, 7, *8*, *9*
obtuse triangles, *127*, 128
offensive play, 125–26
officials, 92–100, *94–100*, 211
offsides, 70, *96*, *97*, *99*
Ohio, STEM schools in, 5–6
Okewole, Ade, 252, 253, 254, 255, 256
Oklahoma City Impact soccer team, 251, 254
Oklahoma City Intruders soccer team, 252, 256
Olivera, Ricardo, 233
on-the-run ball control, 81, *82*
opponents, assessment of, 11
optical illusions, 129–34, *130–33*
out of play balls, 72
outside triangle ball movement, *129*
oxygen, 179

P

pairs, in practice sessions, 184–86
parabolas, 16, *17*
paradox illusions, 130–31, *131*
parallelograms, 136
parents, etiquette for, 247
Parkinson's Law, 240–41
passing
    angles in, *169–70*
    as ball control skill, 58
    described, 65, *66*
    vs. dribbling, 206
    shooting and, 204
Peacock, John Brian, 164, 182, 191–92. *See also* Seventeen Steps

penalty kicks, 69–70, 72, *95*
pentagons, 232
PE (potential energy), 32
perception. *See* senses
perspective, 133–34, *134*
Peter Principle, 238
physical abilities, 10–11, 134, *135*, 152–53. *See also* ball control skills; stamina; strength building
physics
    common equations, *276–79*
    constants in, 36
    defined, 2, 24–26, *26*
    of energy, 32–38
    soccer and, 124
physiological energy/work, 124, 166, 188–94, 240
pitches. *See* fields
planes, inclined, 45–46, *45–46*
plantar fascia, 157, 160–61
players. *See also* field formations; physical abilities
    age of, 102, *103–4*
    ball possession time, 52, 166, 183
    famous names, 233
    groups of, in practice sessions, 164–68, 182–83, 184–87, 200–203
    health considerations, 245–47
    skill level of, 58–59, 244
    space between, 193–94
    team positions, 59–60, 74–76
playing fields. *See* fields
poker chips, 165–66, 209
possession time, 52, 166, 183
postal workers, energy cost calculations, 191
potential energy, 32
practice. *See also* ball control skills; Seventeen Steps
    player activity during, 167–69, 183–84, 196
    player groups in, 164–68, 182–83, 184–87, 200–203
    steps of, *245*

standing around, avoiding, 167–68,
183–84, 196
Stanis, Stephan, 233
stars, visible light from, 37
starting motion, 77, *78*, 196
static equilibrium, 40
Steinbeck, John, 124
STEM educational approach
engineering in, 14–15
mathematics in, 15–16
overview, 2–3, 11–12, 19, 259
science in, 12–13
technology in, 13–14
STEM Education Coalition,
objectives, 3–5
stoppages, during games, 205
stopping
of ball, 184–87
of motion, 196
straddle-and-dribble ball control, 82,
83
strategy development, 200–201, 208,
209
strength building, 197–98
Strickland, Ted, 6
stride length, 134, *135*
substitution, signal for, *96*
success, showing up and, 242–43
Suit, Nick, 250
sunlight, shadows and, 10
Super Eagles soccer team, 56, *57*
sweating, 192–93
sweepers, 74
swimming, 10

T
tackling, 185–86, 200, 203
tactical play, 208
tangents, 225, *225*
targets
for passing/shooting, *169–70*
size of, 203–4, 207
team-building, 91–92
team management principles, 245–49
team positions, 59–60, 74–76. *See also*
field formations
teamwork, 209
technology, in STEM educational
approach, 13–14
temperature
conversion tables, *273*
physiological work and, 192–93
tendons, of feet, 157
Tennessee Technological University
soccer team, 234, *235*
Terrell, Ernie, 251, 252, 253, 254, 255,
256
thermal energy, 32
thigh, in trapping, 45, *46*, 65, *67–68*
third-class levers, 42, *42*
throwing, 185
throw-ins, 62, *96*, *98*, 146
ticket lines, 58
time, shooting distance and, 203
time out, signal for, *99*
time periods, of games, 60
toenail problems, 161
toes, 156
Tonubbee, Mike, 252, 253, 254, 255,
256
tools. *See* machines
Torres, Dara Grace, 10
total quality management (TQM)
in business management, 238–41
soccer case study, 243–44
Total Soccer formations, *173*
tournaments, 233
TQM. *See* total quality management
(TQM)
trajectory models, 33, 108, *109*,
138–41, *140–41*. *See also* bending,
of ball's trajectory
transportation, 246
trapezoid/trapezium, 135–36, *136*
trapping, 58, 64, 65, *67*, 184–87
triangles
acute, *127*, 128
circles and, 221–22
in field formations, 127–29, *129*
inscribed, 227–28, *228*

295